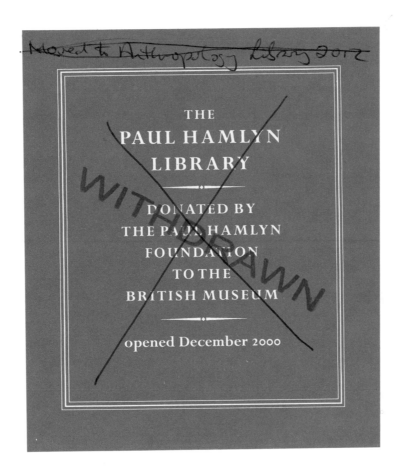

RICHARD E. LEAKEY

Human Origins

Hamish Hamilton

M49353

First published in 1982 by
Hamish Hamilton
Garden House
57–59 Long Acre
London WC2E 9J2

ISBN 0 241 10750 4

This book was designed and produced by
The Rainbird Publishing Group Limited,
36 Park Street, London W1

House Editors: Linda Gamlin, Jo Cheesewright
Designer: Trevor Vincent

Text photoset by SX Composing Limited,
Rayleigh, Essex, England
Colour origination by Bridge Graphics Limited,
Hull, Humberside, England
Printed and bound by Printer Industria Gráfica SA,
Barcelona, Spain

D. L. B. 42353-1981

Contents

Foreword

Fifty years ago no one knew for certain where the early stages of human evolution took place. Remains of human-like creatures had been found in Southeast Asia, in China, in Europe and in southern Africa, but none of these areas could definitely be called the birthplace of our species. Today, there is little doubt that we first emerged in Africa.

That we can be so sure of this is largely due to the work of my father, Louis Leakey, who pioneered the search for early man in East Africa. The son of a missionary, he was born in Kenya in 1903 and made his first archaeological finds – stone tools – when he was twelve years old. Although he came to England to attend school and then University, he spent most of his life in Africa hunting for fossils of our ancestors.

With my mother Mary, an Englishwoman who first travelled out to Africa in 1935, he made a great number of significant finds, particularly at Olduvai Gorge in Tanzania. Together they explored this deep, dry gorge tirelessly, year after year, and by the time my father died in 1972 it had yielded more information about our distant past than any other prehistoric site in the world. My mother still works at Olduvai Gorge today, as well as at the nearby site of Laetoli where, in 1978, a dramatic discovery was made – a set of hominid footprints, left almost four million years ago in a layer of volcanic rock.

Like my brothers, Philip and Jonathan, I was taken on fossil-hunting expeditions by my parents almost as soon as I could walk. I knew how to identify fossils and stone tools at an early age as well as learning how to survive, unarmed and without food, in the African bush. Although as a young man I decided not to follow in my parents'

footsteps, eventually I realized that I shared their fascination for discovering more about human origins. From 1967 onwards, I participated in a number of palaeontological expeditions, and for over ten years I have worked with a research team at Koobi Fora in northern Kenya. This site, on the eastern shore of Lake Turkana, is particularly rich in hominid fossils and, with the invaluable help of my wife Meave, I have been fortunate enough to uncover some interesting new evidence about our early ancestors.

This book is a summary, not just of my own discoveries and those of my parents, but of the many important finds made by palaeoanthropologists throughout the world. Our field of research has undergone tremendous advances in the past decade and for the first time we can confidently put forward a scheme of human evolution that is based largely on solid evidence. I have tried here to describe how this evidence has been obtained, and how it has been interpreted to gradually piece together a picture of our past.

Many friends and colleagues have provided information and ideas that are included in this book and I should like to thank them all for their contributions, particularly Bernard Wood whose help and advice have been extremely valuable. Kamoya Kimeu and Glynn Isaac have worked closely with me at Koobi Fora and to them I am especially grateful. I also wish to thank Linda Gamlin who has put in many long hours of editorial work from which the book has benefited greatly. My wife Meave has been of tremendous assistance in seeing this book to completion and I remain, as always, in her debt.

Richard Leakey.

Chapter One

Special animals called humans

Tales of the past

When I was a child, I loved to listen to my father telling stories of his childhood; of the animals that were always around his mud-and-thatch house, of the games he played with the local Kikuyu children and of the journeys he made to Nairobi, a mere eight miles from his home, which never took less than a day. These journeys were made on foot along narrow paths which led from one village to the next, so that the journey was frequently interrupted to make visits to friends on the way. Nairobi in those days was only a collection of small buildings clustered around the railway station, nothing like the modern city that today is Kenya's capital.

Children and adults everywhere share this fascination for tales of the past. Parents, grandparents and great-grandparents relate stories of their childhood. Legends and sagas of dramatic events are passed down from one generation to another. Books and plays written long ago also tell us a great deal about life in years gone by.

If we deliberately set out to find out what we can about the past we will be able to discover quite a lot about recent times, less about what happened 500 years ago, and less again about what happened 1,000 years ago.

Before about 3000 BC there were no true written records, so it is much more difficult to find out what happened. It is here that the archaeologist steps in. From the items found during excavations of early villages, towns and ports, archaeologists can guess how past peoples must have lived. The items they find will generally include buildings, farming implements and other tools, weapons, ornaments, pottery, jewelry and coins. All these items can tell the archaeologist something about how their owners lived.

But people did not always have jewelry, coins, weapons and pottery. They did not always live in buildings. Very early people had few possessions, and

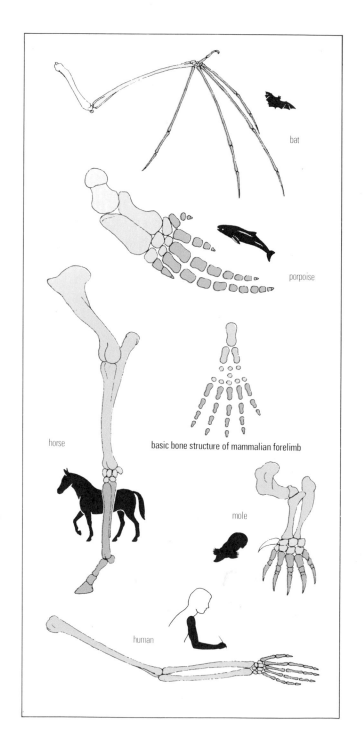

bat

porpoise

horse

basic bone structure of mammalian forelimb

mole

human

those they did have were probably made of natural materials such as wood, animal skins, plant fibres and tree bark. Such materials decay and disappear with time, so the archaeologist of today has no hope of finding them. When we look at these very early people we have to turn to the scanty evidence of stone tools and bones that are preserved in the rocks as fossils.

If we go far enough back in time, we find that the people were different; their fossilized bones are not quite the same as our bones. The further back we go, the more different they look from us. This gradual change in living things is called evolution and it applies to every animal and plant on the earth today.

What is evolution?

At one time, many people believed that the animals and plants that we see in the world today were created all at once by God. We now know that all these animals and plants only appeared gradually, and that the first living things were very small and simple and were related to present-day bacteria. From these simple forms of life all other living things developed. This happened very slowly, taking over 3,000 million years. This process of change and development is what is meant by evolution and it is still going on today, although it is so gradual that we would not notice any changes during a lifetime.

Evolution explains why animals have so many things in common. The foreleg of a frog or a crocodile, the wing of a bird, the front flipper of a whale and the

Because they evolved from a common ancestor all mammals have much the same basic skeleton, although it is modified to suit the particular way of life of each species. The fundamental pattern of bones found in the forelimb is shown in the centre of the diagram. This basic pattern is seen clearly in humans, whose hands are not adapted to any specific task, but it is harder to see the pattern in the horse, which has become adapted to fast running. To give it extra speed the limbs have grown very long, and to strengthen them the 'fingers' are joined together to form one very thick bone. In the bat the bones of the forelimb are elongated to carry the skin that forms the wing, while in sea mammals, such as the porpoise, the forelimb acts as a paddle and is short and squat for greater efficiency in swimming. To increase its digging power the mole has developed thick, strong forelimbs and a sixth 'finger' (shown here in white) but apart from this extra digit the mole's bones follow the same pattern as other mammals. A similar pattern can also be seen in the legs of frogs and lizards, and in the wings of birds, since all land vertebrates (amphibians, reptiles, birds and mammals) ultimately share a common ancestor.

arm of a human being all have the same basic bone structure. The fossils that we find explain how these structures developed from the fins of early fishes. The first fish which crawled onto the land had a similar basic bone structure and from these fish evolved the amphibians, reptiles, birds and mammals of today.

We need to explain three things to understand evolution. First, why do animals and plants need to change? Second, how do these changes come about? And third, how do the changes get passed on from one generation to the next?

Change or perish

Human beings are now becoming aware that food and fuel are in limited supply. We must 'adapt', that is, change the way we live in order to conserve the resources we need. More efficient engines, better insulated houses and more productive use of farmland are all part of our conscious attempts at adaptation.

Animals and plants face similar problems of survival but they don't solve them by thinking about them as we do. Changes in weather cause changes in temperature which affect all animals and plants everywhere. The world is constantly changing. Those animals which can adapt to the changes will do better than those which cannot. Because every animal must compete with other animals, those which are best at finding food and escaping from enemies will survive, while those which are less successful at these things will die. To survive the constant changes in environment, animals must not only be able to take advantage of present conditions: they must also be capable of adapting to new conditions.

How does change come about?

The evolution of living things which are better suited to their environment, or to new conditions, depends on the fact that the offspring are never exact copies of their parents. What happens is this: the parents pass on a set of instructions which determines what the offspring looks like. The instructions are known as *genes* and the offspring gets a mixture of genes from both parents. That is why you may have the same colour eyes as your mother, but wavy hair like your father.

In the mixing-up process a 'mistake' can occur and one or two of the instructions are altered. These mistakes are known as *mutations* and it is a matter of chance whether the new instructions they produce are better or worse. The mutation may put the

of the 'natural' alteration of a few instructions and the 'selection' which happens because animals with improved characters have more offspring. Because they have more offspring, more of the improved characters are passed on to future generations.

Natural selection does to wild animals what animal breeders can do to domesticated animals, although natural selection works much more slowly. The many different breeds of dog which we see today are the result of many hundreds of years of breeding

Animal breeders have produced this breed of miniature horses (shown here with a carthorse for comparison) by selecting small horses to breed from, then selecting the smallest of their offspring to breed from again, and so on for a large number of generations. What animal breeders do to domestic animals is very similar to what natural selection does in the wild, but they are able to achieve results much more quickly because they can select only the 'best' animals at each generation and exclude all the others. Natural selection takes much longer because it is much more haphazard – chance plays a large part and in spite of their advantages the 'best' animals may sometimes die young.

A python approaches a group of vervet monkeys on the African savanna. One monkey has already noticed the snake and will probably escape, but the other monkeys calmly continue feeding. An inattentive or slow-running monkey is likely to be killed by predators at an early age, whereas a wary and fast-moving monkey will tend to survive, and therefore has more chance of producing a large number of young. As a result it will tend to pass more of its genes on to the next generation than other monkeys do and the characteristics which helped it to survive will become more widespread. This is the basis of the process known as natural selection which Charles Darwin recognized as the driving force of evolution.

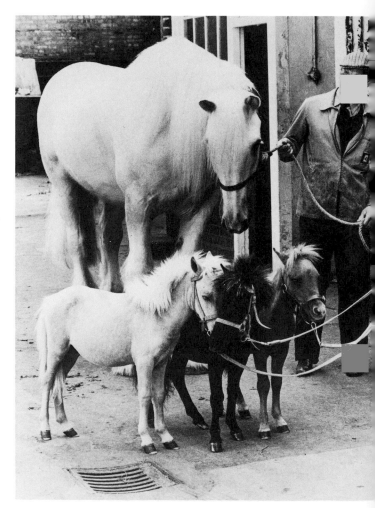

animal or plant (known as a *mutant*) at a serious disadvantage so that it dies or does not do as well as its parents. But sometimes the change is a lucky one and the new instructions lead to an improvement: for some it may be having slightly longer legs to run faster, for others having stronger jaws to crunch harder foods. If these improvements mean that they can run faster to evade predators, or eat different sorts of food, then the 'new' animals are more likely to survive and flourish.

Because such animals have a better chance of breeding and bringing up their young, scientists say that they are 'fitter' than their competitors. The idea of *fitness* and *competition* is the basis of Charles Darwin's theory of *natural selection*. The theory is called natural selection because it is the combination from the same basic dog stock. Breeders pick out of each generation the animals with the features they are trying to develop, and then breed more dogs from these. By choosing small dogs they have been able to produce tiny breeds like the Chihuahua, and by choosing large dogs they have produced breeds like the Great Dane and the Irish Wolfhound. The same is true for all domestic animals and that is why there are so many breeds of farm animals and crops today.

Our closest relatives

Human beings, like all other forms of life today, are the result of millions of years of evolution. Sixty million years ago, when all mammals were rather primitive, one group changed: instead of living on the ground they moved into the trees where competition from other animals was much less. The eyesight of these mammals improved and the eyes became forward-facing and moved closer together so that they had stereoscopic vision. This made it easier for them to judge distance, so that they could safely leap from one branch to another. They developed fingers and toes and a relatively large brain. The number of babies produced at each birth was reduced so that the mother could carry her offspring around with her. All these features made it easier for them to live safely in the trees. This group of mammals have since evolved into the modern primates, such as the bushbabies, lemurs, monkeys, apes and humans. These primates still share the original characters which evolved to help their ancestors inhabit the tree tops. Human beings, however, have evolved in a rather different way from other primates and we have a number of features which separate us readily from all other primate groups. What are these special human features which make us so different from our primate relatives?

This diagram shows a possible family tree for the primates, the order of mammals to which we belong. Some of the details about how the tree 'branches' are just guesswork. The primates are thought to have split off from the insectivores (the order that includes shrews and hedgehogs) about seventy million years ago.

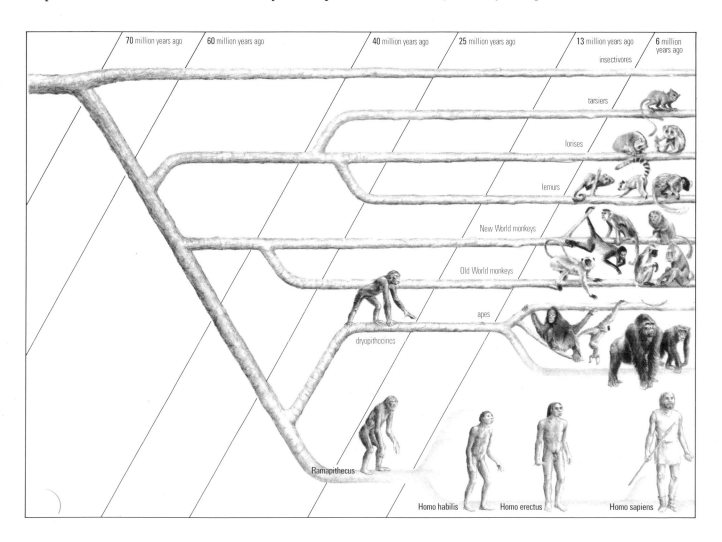

70 million years ago   60 million years ago   40 million years ago   25 million years ago   13 million years ago   6 million years ago

insectivores

tarsiers

lorises

lemurs

New World monkeys

Old World monkeys

apes

dryopithecines

Ramapithecus

Homo habilis   Homo erectus   Homo sapiens

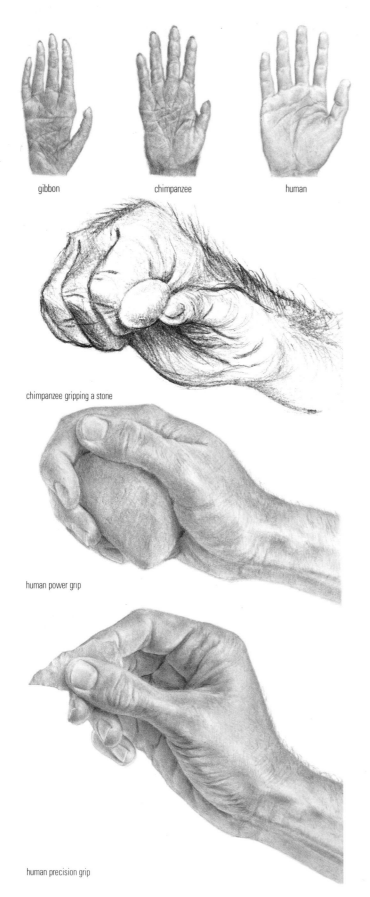

gibbon   chimpanzee   human

chimpanzee gripping a stone

human power grip

human precision grip

Standing on our own two feet

One of our main advantages is that we can stand on our hindlegs and move around with our bodies held upright. This does not mean we can run faster but it does mean that our arms and hands are free to do other things. Because our hands do not have to bear the weight of our bodies, they have become very mobile and capable of delicate movements. Our fingers are so sensitive that we can tell what we are touching with our eyes closed. We now use this dexterity for doing things like writing and playing the piano, but it was probably developed in the first place to help our ancestors gather and prepare food. Their strong but delicate fingers could pick berries, dig roots out of tiny holes and crevices, and even remove the tough peel of fruits to reach the delicious edible part inside.

Just as our hands are special, so are our feet. They are specially shaped and stiff enough to support our weight, to stop us toppling over and to give us a good push-off when we run or jump. But as well as being a good platform and springboard, they are flexible enough to adjust to walking over uneven surfaces, like farmtracks, stony footpaths or stepping-stones.

Recalling the past and planning the future

Two things are important about brains: how big they are and how they are organized. It is not just the size of the brain that is important, but how big it is in relation to the body. If we compare the size of our brains with those of other mammals whose bodies are about the same size as ours, we find that the human brain is the largest. So it would seem that only part of our brain is needed to control the body, and the rest is free to do other things. In some simple animals the brain just stops and starts muscles. In

We can do far more with our hands than any other primate, since we do not need to use them for locomotion. The gibbon must have very long hands for gripping branches as it swimgs through the trees and the chimpanzee needs its hands for support while walking – it folds its fingers under and takes the weight of its body on its knuckles. Only human hands have a structure that allows the tip of the forefinger and thumb to come together in a 'precision grip' – the chimpanzee's attempt at this is very clumsy, as shown by the drawing of a chimpanzee gripping a stone. The precision grip allowed the fine manipulation of stone tools, as in cutting up food, while the power grip was useful to our ancestors for less delicate tasks, such as making stone tools or breaking open bones with a pebble.

10

A group of !Kung people, modern-day hunter-gatherers who live on the fringes of the Kalahari Desert in southern Africa, assemble at their evening camp to sing, tell stories and discuss the day's events. They will also tell each other if they have seen a good place to collect food, and they will make plans for the next day. If the supplies of game and plant foods in the area are running low they may decide to leave this camp-site and walk on a few miles to a new spot. To survive as hunter-gatherers they must *be able to talk to each other and the same was probably true for our ancestors, who lived in a very similar way millions of years ago.*

humans, parts of the brain also do just this, but one area, which is called the cerebral cortex, does more complicated things. It does all the things a computer can do, like solving mathematical problems, but it can also do things a computer cannot do. The cortex allows us to set ourselves problems and develop new ideas. We can plan the future and we can recall past experiences. It is this capacity of the human brain that explains its large size relative to our bodies.

The special place of language

Of all the special features of humans, spoken language is probably the most important. Although other animals can signal simple messages to each other, human language goes much further than this. With hundreds and hundreds of words to choose from we can send much more complicated messages.

This allows humans to discuss important matters and plan ahead. We have evidence that our ancestors lived in bands and shared their food. Some members of the band probably collected fruits, nuts and roots, while others hunted animals. At the end of the day, everyone brought their food back to a base camp where it was shared out. We can guess that they needed to talk to each other to decide when they would meet up again. It would also enable them to tell each other if they had seen a tree full of fruit or a herd of animals somewhere nearby. When a group of them hunted a fairly large animal, language must have been useful in working out their hunting tactics beforehand.

Tools and technology

One important human characteristic, that marks us out from other animals, is the way we make and use tools. A few animals use very simple tools: sea otters use stones to break open shells, for example, and chimpanzees use twigs to extract termites from the ground. But these 'tools' are basically natural objects that the animals have found a use for. Usually they use the object just as it is, and even if they adapt it for their use the changes made are very small: the chimpanzee, for example, takes a twig, removes the leaves, and breaks it into a suitable size and shape, but that is all. When a human being turns a natural object into a tool, far greater changes are made to it, and the finished product often looks nothing like the raw material. No animal makes tools in the imaginative way that humans do.

The simplest tools which early people used were made by knocking chips off a stone to produce sharp flakes. These simple stone tools could be used effectively to cut up dead animals, and are still used by some people today. I have often made a simple

woodpecker finch

chimpanzee

Egyptian vulture

sea otter

A few animals use tools – the woodpecker finch, found in the Galapagos Islands, uses a cactus spine to prise insects out of wood; the sea otter cracks open shellfish by placing them on its chest and hitting them with a stone; the Egyptian vulture drops stones onto ostrich eggs to break their shells; and the chimpanzee extracts termites from their nest with a long twig.

stone tool in this way when I have to cut something and I don't have a knife handy. As our ancestors became more skilful they learned to make more specialized tools such as harpoons, fish hooks and knives. With these they could be better hunters and even start making clothes and building houses and boats. Today we have developed technology to the point where we can make highly complex tools like computers, lasers, space satellites and electron microscopes.

A long childhood

Unlike most other animals, humans live in family groups and take a long time to grow up to the point where they can look after themselves. Human babies, that are a few weeks or even months old, are helpless. Most week-old animals can walk and run but human babies don't learn to do this until they are more than one year old. Young animals can generally obtain food for themselves a few months after birth but human children, if left to their own devices in the wild, would be incapable of doing this until six or seven years of age. Because human babies take so long to become independent they must be looked after for several years, and humans live in family groups in order to care for their children.

A long childhood is an important part of being human, because we are essentially *cultural* animals. While we are growing up we are busy learning all the complicated ideas and skills we will need for our lives as adults in a human world, as well as the customs and manners which govern human behaviour.

One people

These special characteristics which make us human are shared by us all, whether we live in an igloo in the cold north, in a mud-and-thatch hut in the tropics, or in a skyscraper in any of our modern cities. We all share a common ancestry which has led to the most unique of our characteristics: our ability to adapt our environment to suit ourselves. This ability has enabled us to inhabit every part of the earth from the coldest to the hottest. People have lived for months on the bottom of the ocean, and have even travelled thousands of kilometres into space to land on the moon.

But with all our technology, we now have the power to destroy our planet and all life on it. It is my hope that an understanding of our past, and an appreciation of our common heritage, will help us to preserve and develop the world for a better future.

Chapter Two

The secrets of the rocks

The search for clues

My childhood was spent in various remote areas of East Africa, in Kenya and Tanzania, where my parents were searching for evidence of our ancestors. For many months they searched the fossil sites on the islands and shores of Lake Victoria. At other times I remember chasing sheets of cellophane blowing away in the wind as my mother laboriously traced the art of our ancestors in rock shelters in Tanzania. But perhaps the most exciting times of all were at Olduvai Gorge on the Serengeti Plains where wild animals were a natural part of our everyday life.

Since then I have continued searching for evidence of the past in my own career, and I have experienced for myself the thrill of finding a complete skull of one of our ancestors, two million years old.

An aerial view of the East African Rift Valley which runs from Turkey in the north, along the Red Sea and through East Africa to end in Mozambique. The Rift Valley marks a weakness in the earth's crust where many large cracks, or faults, have appeared. Lakes and volcanoes dot the Valley floor and it is an excellent place for finding the fossilized remains of our ancestors.

The cracking of Africa

I was very fortunate to be born in Kenya, for Kenya has running through it the East African Rift Valley. This exceptional geological feature has led to the formation of numerous fossil sites during the last twenty million years, the period of time when humans evolved from primitive ape-like animals into the intelligent creatures that we are today.

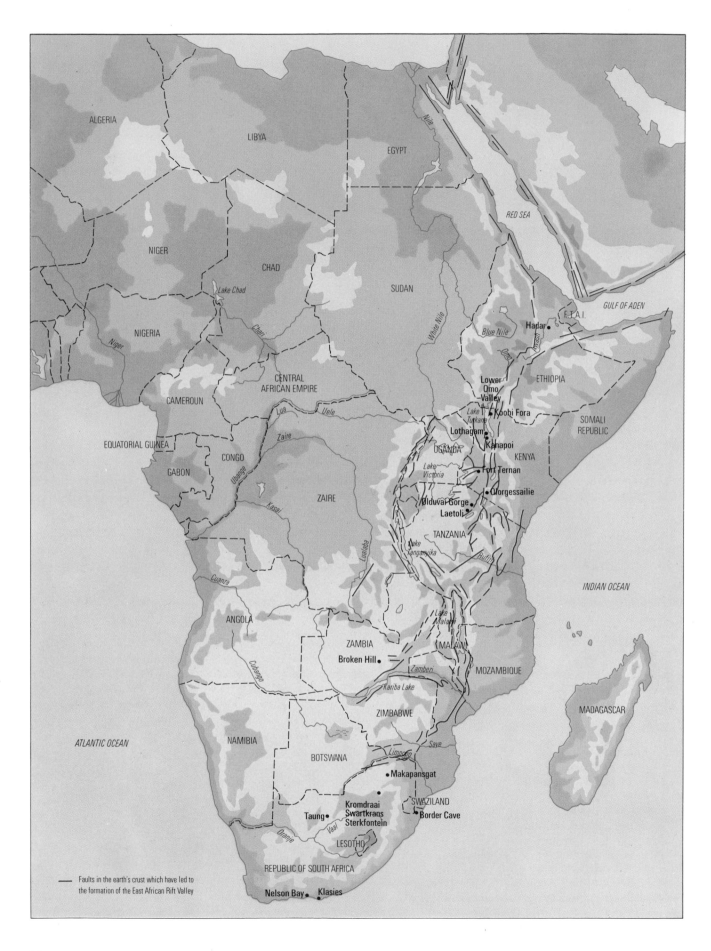

ALGERIA

LIBYA

EGYPT

NIGER

CHAD

SUDAN

Nile

RED SEA

Lake Chad

Chari

Niger

NIGERIA

CENTRAL
AFRICAN EMPIRE

White Nile

Blue Nile

Hadar •

E.T.A.I.

GULF OF ADEN

CAMEROUN

Lua

Uele

Omo

Lower
Omo
Valley

ETHIOPIA

EQUATORIAL GUINEA

Zaire

Ubange

CONGO

*Lake
Turkana*

• Koobi Fora

SOMALI
REPUBLIC

GABON

Lothagem •

• Kanapoi

Kasai

ZAIRE

UGANDA

KENYA

*Lake
Victoria*

• Fort Ternan

Lualaba

Olduvai Gorge •

• Olorgessailie

Laetoli •

*Lake
Tanganyika*

TANZANIA

Rufiji

INDIAN OCEAN

Cuanza

ANGOLA

*Lake
Malawi*

ZAMBIA

Broken Hill •

MALAWI

MADAGASCAR

Cubango

Zambezi

MOZAMBIQUE

Kariba Lake

ATLANTIC OCEAN

ZIMBABWE

NAMIBIA

Save

BOTSWANA

Limpopo

• Makapansgat

SWAZILAND

Kromdraai
Swartkrans
Sterkfontein

Taung •

• Border Cave

Vaal

Orange

LESOTHO

REPUBLIC OF SOUTH AFRICA

Nelson Bay •   • Klasies

— Faults in the earth's crust which have led to
the formation of the East African Rift Valley

The East African Rift Valley marks an area of weakness in the earth's surface, that runs through Africa, from the Red Sea in the north to Mozambique in the south. Flying over the Valley in an aeroplane one sees the sides rising, sometimes as much as 2,000 metres (6,600 feet) above its floor. In places the Valley is as much as 80 kilometres (50 miles) wide; it is lined with huge cliffs and escarpments, and dotted with volcanoes surrounded by vast black lava flows.

Twenty million years ago, however, this huge rift was only a shallow depression marked by lakes and volcanoes. As the depression gradually deepened, cracks began to form in the earth's surface, creating the cliffs and escarpments we see today.

While these massive movements were taking place, other events were happening which were important for the preservation of clues about our past. As the lakes formed in the Rift Valley depression, rivers began to wash away soil and rocks from the newly formed hills on either side. This soil was carried down the hills by the rivers and later dumped on flood plains and deltas, and in the lakes themselves. In these places sediments of sand, silt and clay gradually built up, and any bones of dead animals lying in these areas became buried and preserved as fossils. Among the animals which were preserved in this way were some of our ancestors.

These geological processes have continued in the Rift Valley over the past twenty million years, so that many layers of sediment and fossilized bones have been built up. In some places these are hundreds of metres thick. Often the layers of sediment and the fossilized bones have remained buried, but in some areas movements of the earth's crust have continued and caused them to be uplifted. When this happens they in their turn become eroded by rivers, which cut through the layers of rock like a cake and expose the fossilized bones. It is in these places that, with careful searching, we can find many clues from the distant past.

The earliest fossils of human ancestors are found in Africa, and this map shows the major sites where they have been found. Many of the sites are associated with the East African Rift Valley where ideal conditions for the fossilization of animal and hominid bones have long existed. Over the last twenty million years the Valley has gradually deepened and rivers and streams have eroded soil from the highlands along its sides. This soil has been deposited in the Valley and layer upon layer of sedimentary rock has slowly built up. Our ancestors often chose to camp beside streams or lakes and as a result many hominid remains are found in the rocks.

How to get preserved as a fossil

Unfortunately the chances of any animal becoming a fossil are not very great, and the chances of a fossil then being discovered many thousands of years later are even less. It is not surprising that of all the millions of animals that have lived in the past, we actually have fossils of only a very few.

There are several ways in which animals and plants may become fossilized. First, it is essential that the remains are buried. Dead animals and plants are quickly destroyed if they remain exposed to the air. Plants rot, while scavengers, such as hyaenas, eat the flesh and bones of animals. Hyaenas love to crunch the bones, while beetles, flies and grubs consume all edible parts that are left. Finally, the few remaining bones soon disintegrate in the hot sun and pouring rain. If buried in suitable conditions, however, animal and plant remains will be preserved. The same chemicals which change sand and silt into hard rock will also enter the animal or plant remains and make them hard too. When this happens we say that they have become fossilized. Usually only the bones of an animal and the toughest part of a plant are preserved.

The soft body parts of an animal or the fine fibres of a leaf may occasionally become fossilized, but they must be buried very quickly for this to happen. It may sometimes occur with river and lake sediments but is much more likely to happen with volcanic ash. One site near Lake Victoria, where my parents worked, contained many thousands of beautifully preserved insects, spiders, seeds, twigs, roots and leaves. A nearby volcano must have erupted very suddenly, burying everything in a layer of ash. The insects had no time to escape before they were smothered.

As we have seen, river and lake sediments preserve a great many bones, but caves are another site where fossils are easily formed and luckily our ancestors left many clues in caves which make convenient shelters and homes. Things that people brought in as food or tools were left on the cave floor, and mud, sand, and other debris washed in by rivers and rain buried them.

Detective work with rocks

When we find a fossil site, it is important to extract from it the maximum amount of information. First we study the rocks, or the geology. By looking at rocks, geologists can tell what they are composed of and this tells them how they were formed. Rocks made of lava were formed in volcanic eruptions, for

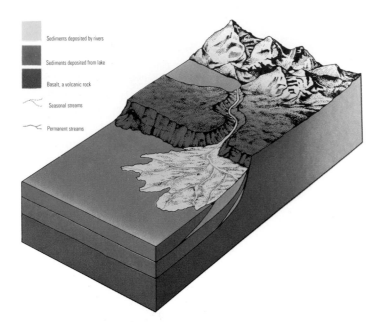

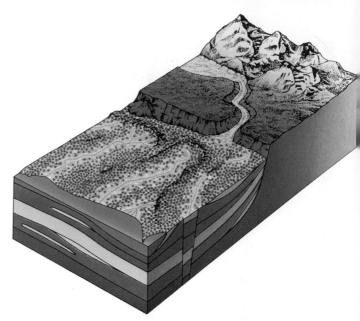

Part of the eastern shore of Lake Turkana as it may have looked about two million years ago. Rivers draining from the Ethiopian highlands (shown in the distance) flowed into a major river which in turn flowed into Lake Turkana. The silt it carried was deposited as a delta, shown in yellow on the diagram. Other layers of sediment were deposited from the lake waters themselves: the red layers on the diagram represent these sediments.

The same area today. The river which once flowed into Lake Turkana is now dry for most of the year. The waters of the lake are low and the sediments around it are being eroded by seasonal streams. These create a landscape of gulleys and ridges among the sedimentary rocks and expose fossils that were buried thousands or millions of years ago. The spit of sand on which the Koobi Fora base camp is sited can be seen in the foreground.

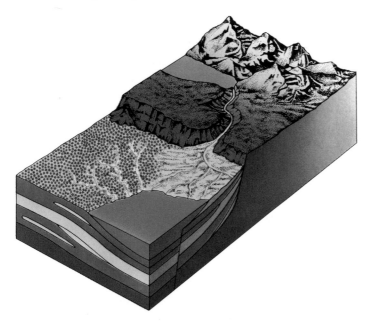

The same area about one million years later, when the lake was much smaller. The delta and lake sediments have continued to build up at times when the lake level was high. At times when it fell, large areas of sediment were exposed and were eroded by seasonal streams flowing across them. Movements of the earth's crust associated with the formation of the East African Rift Valley caused the sediments to buckle and arch upwards, and at various times faults appeared – these are shown by vertical lines on the diagram. These faults make an already complicated picture even more difficult for geologists to untangle.

example. Rocks made of silt and sand were laid down by rivers or lakes and are called sedimentary rocks. Geologists can also say something about the conditions when sedimentary rocks were deposited. We all know the difference between the sticky mud on the bottom of a pond or pool and the coarse sand of a fast-flowing river: when these harden they form different types of rock.

When we have studied the geology we can begin to collect the fossils. Fossils tell us about the various kinds of animals that were living at the time when the sediments were laid down and these in turn tell us about the environment. If the animals were mainly antelopes then the environment was probably savanna, but if there were a lot of monkeys and few antelopes, it was probably forest. Shells, fish, crocodiles and hippos tell us that there was a lake. Plants and trees also become fossilized. Tree trunks, leaves, seeds and roots indicate the type of vegetation. And we can also learn a lot about the countryside by searching the rock for fossil pollen. By comparing the fossil pollen with pollen collected from present-day grasses, shrubs and trees, we can get an idea of the sort of vegetation that was growing many thousands or even millions of years ago.

The study of fossilized animals and plants is called *palaeontology*.

A fossilized fragment of a crocodile's jaw, found among the dry, scorched rocks to the east of Lake Turkana, shows that the lake once covered a much wider area.

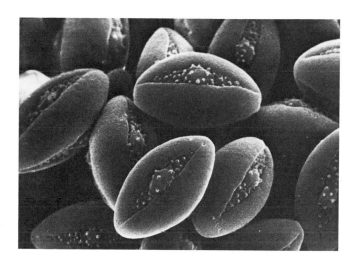

Pollen grains of the horse chestnut tree seen under an electron microscope. Pollen grains always have distinctive shape and surface patterns, which identify the species of plant they came from. They are also very hard and resistant so they survive for millions of years. This is extremely useful to palaeontologists who can extract pollen grains from sedimentary rock and use them to discover what sort of plants are growing, and thus what the climate was like, when those sediments were deposited.

How are prehistoric sites found?

As we have seen fossils are formed in places where animal and plant remains are quickly buried, such as on the flood plains and deltas of rivers, on the shores of lakes, in caves and on the slopes of active volcanoes. But most fossils stay buried for ever under hundreds of metres of sediments. To be discovered the fossils must be exposed by erosion of the layers of sediment which bury them.

The Rift Valley is an area where movement of the earth's crust not only caused the remains of ancient animals to be buried, but also caused them to be exposed again. There are many areas of the world where similar movements are occurring. Another important example is in the foothills of the Himalayas. Here, over the past fifteen million years, rivers have been eroding the mountains and depositing enormous quantities of silt in the foothills. Many layers of sediments, which in places are 6 kilometres (almost 20,000 feet) thick, have been formed and the remains of many ancient animals have been buried. More recently, these layers have been uplifted so that they are now being eroded, exposing the fossilized bones of the ancient animals. Many remains of our earliest ancestors have been discovered in these sediments in the Siwalik Hills, Pakistan.

Similar processes have also occurred in other parts of the world, but in only a few of these do we find evidence of our past. The last twenty million years, the period during which our ancestors evolved, is only a small amount of time compared to the earth's long 4,500 million years of history, so there are very few rocks of the right age. Where the rocks are of the right age, not all will hold the clues we are looking for, because our ancestors only lived in a few areas of Africa, Asia, and Europe where the climate and environment were suitable. Consequently the number of places where they might have left their remains as fossils is small.

The difficult job of finding fossils

In the region to the east of Lake Turkana in northern Kenya, where I have been working for more than ten years, fossils are found in sediments which cover thousands of square kilometres. Here nearly all the fossil discoveries have been made by a team of sharp-eyed Kenyans, led by Kamoya Kimeu. Kamoya and his team leave camp early in the morning, before the sun is up, and drive to a pre-selected spot by Land Rover. As the sun rises, they move out over the sediments, walking up gullies beside dry streambeds,

Every day at sunrise, a team led by Kamoya Kimeu sets out to walk across the stark sedimentary rocks near Lake Turkana in search of fossils.

Fossils become exposed as rain and wind erode the sedimentary rock in which they are buried. Only occasionally do the fossil prospectors at Lake Turkana come across hominid remains such as these million-year-old fragments of a Homo erectus *skull.*

clambering over boulders and constantly searching. Every bone they see is examined, although most of them turn out to be unimportant. But sometimes they are lucky and they find a complete jaw of an extinct pig or the skull of a hyaena. On very rare occasions they will find the remains of one of our ancestors and then there is much cause for celebration.

As the morning progresses, the sun gets hotter and brighter until by midday they have to stop and rest under the shade of a thorn tree, quench their thirst and eat a little lunch. Later in the afternoon, when the heat and glare of the sun have lessened, they will continue the search.

At other sites, thousands of fossils may be found in a small area of sediment. These sorts of sites have to be excavated carefully and the bones removed one by one. Drawings are made to show how the bones were lying as this will often help in working out how they came to be in that spot.

Evidence from human litter

We have talked about fossils as clues to our past, but there is also a lot of other evidence. Fortunately our ancestors were not especially tidy and we can find the litter that they left behind where they lived and ate: this litter tells us a lot about their way of life.

An archaeologist is a scientist whose job it is to study this type of evidence. The sorts of tools, the bones of the animals that were eaten, and the variety of places in which our ancestors left their refuse all help to reconstruct their way of life.

Archaeological sites are always carefully excavated since a great deal can be learned from the way this litter is distributed. When our ancestors made a stone tool, pieces of stone were scattered around them. It seems that they often left the fragments they did not need lying on the ground, just where they fell. By carefully noting the position of each piece and then trying to fit the pieces together again, archaeologists can learn a lot about how stone tools were made. Fossilized bone fragments can sometimes be fitted together in the same sort of way, and from them we can tell that our ancestors broke open bones to get at the marrow.

Dating bones and stones

Fossilized bones are usually found in sedimentary rocks which have been laid down by rivers and lakes. Because the layers are laid successively, one on top of another, those at the bottom are always older than the layers at the top. Although this tells us whether a fossil found in a particular layer is older than another, it does not tell us how old the fossil or layer actually is in years.

To find out the age of fossils in numbers of years, we need to know *when* and not just in what order the rocks were formed. By looking at the chemicals in the rocks, it is sometimes possible to tell *when* they were formed. Certain chemicals in the rocks and in the fossils themselves change over a long period of time. For example, some rocks contain a lot of a metal called potassium. Most of this is ordinary potassium and stays in the rocks unchanged. But a small proportion of it is slightly different and gradually changes into a gas called argon. We know how long it takes for this 'special' potassium to change into argon and it always changes at the same rate. If we measure how much of the 'special' potassium is left in the rocks and how much has been changed into argon, we can calculate how many years have gone by since the rock was first formed. This method is particularly useful for dating volcanic rocks which are rich in potassium, but it can only be used for rocks that are older than half-a-million years.

Great care must be taken in excavating any archaeological site. The area is first marked off into squares using pegs and string, and then the area within each square is excavated in stages, a layer at a time, each layer to a specific depth, say 2.5 cm (1 inch). Any items of interest are carefully removed and the exact spot where they were found recorded. Finally, the sand and earth that have been scraped away are sieved to retrieve very small particles. When the whole site has been excavated in this way a plan is drawn up showing where different items were found – this plan shows the 'scatter' of objects which can tell us a great deal about how the site was formed thousands or millions of years ago.

To date fossils from rocks *younger* than 120,000 years, we can use a similar method but one which measures the amount of carbon in the fossils. Bones, like all living things, contain carbon. Some of this carbon breaks down in the same way as the 'special' potassium, but much more quickly. After about 50,000 years so much of it has disappeared that it is very difficult to measure accurately how much is left. A complex process of chemical analysis is required to measure the age of a fossil over 50,000 years old by this method, but it can be done as long as it is less than 120,000 years old. After 120,000 years the minute amount of carbon that remains cannot be measured by the methods used at present, although new techniques are being developed which may make it possible.

Another way we can date the fossils is to look at the bones of other animals found with them. When we look at the fossil record we find certain periods of time during which some animals changed steadily and progressively from one type to another. In Africa the pig family did just this over the last five million years. There were several species of pig at any one time but they were all evolving in the same sort of way. One important feature which changed was their teeth: gradually the back teeth (the molars) got larger, while the teeth in front of them (the pre-molars) grew smaller. The sort of pig teeth we find at a site can therefore tell us how old that site is. What we do is to match them up with teeth from another site, where accurate chemical dating is possible because there are layers of volcanic rock containing the 'special' potassium. If the teeth are the same, the two sites must be about the same age.

The human detective story

These are some of the ways in which we find and interpret clues from our past. There is a special excitement about the search for remains of our ancestors, whether this involves long hours searching in the hot sun, days crouching over a dusty, windswept excavation, or weeks of tedious experiments in a laboratory. When new evidence is found the thrill is worth everything.

The story of our evolution is rather like a detective story, full of clues and uncertainties. But each year more of the clues are found and more uncertainties are settled. It is a fascinating and exciting story in which the detectives are scientists working in a great variety of subjects, and the clues appear in a number of guises. In the next chapter I will begin to relate this story.

Chapter Three

In the beginning

The earliest apes

Our story has a very hazy beginning about thirty million years ago, when a small animal, which is believed to have given rise to both human beings and apes, appeared in the fossil record. This distant ancestor has been called *Aegyptopithecus* and at first glance it seems an unlikely candidate because it looks rather like a small dog. But it had a number of characteristics typical of early primates: it lived in forests, it probably ate fruit and it moved about on all fours in the tree tops, much as monkeys do today.

Nothing is known of the descendants of *Aegyptopithecus* until about twenty million years ago when other primates appear in the fossil record which look much more like modern apes. It was these animals, called the dryopithecines, that my parents were searching for at the fossil sites on the islands and shores of Lake Victoria when I was a child.

This reconstruction shows what a typical dryopithecine may have looked like. These animals probably moved through the trees on all fours as modern monkeys do, eating fruit and leaves.

Plenty of dryopithecine remains are found at these sites, and they vary greatly in size: there were probably as many species of these primitive apes then as there are species of monkeys today. At that time thick forests covered much of Africa and Eurasia (Europe and Asia) and the dryopithecines were relatively common animals. They must have fed on the abundant fruits, leaves, shoots and flowers that were to be found in the forests, and they probably moved on all fours as *Aegyptopithecus* had done.

Twenty million years ago, a map of the world would have looked very different from today. Africa was surrounded by water and was therefore completely separated from Eurasia. But between eighteen million and sixteen million years ago, Africa became connected to Eurasia and animals were able to move freely backwards and forwards between the continents. This meant there was a lot of competition between species, as well as new opportunities for species moving into new environments. These conditions encourage evolutionary change.

The move to open country

At about the same time, the world's climate changed and the immense tropical forests began to disappear. It became cooler and drier and many of the forests gave way to woodland and grassy plains. The dryopithecines had to adapt to the changing environment or become extinct. Many did die out but others began to live on the edge of the forest giving rise to a new group which are called the ramapithecines.

The ramapithecines have larger flatter cheek teeth and smaller front teeth than the dryopithecines. These enabled them to eat the tougher and perhaps less nutritious food which is found on forest edges and in open woodland. Ramapithecines are thought to be the group from which our ancestors evolved. They flourished in Africa, Asia and Europe between fourteen million and eight million years ago, but it is from fossil-bearing rocks in the Siwalik Hills in

(Above) *In the reddish earth of the Siwalik Hills, Pakistan, the bones of animals we now call ramapithecines were buried between fourteen and eight million years ago.*

Several different reconstructions of Ramapithecus – *these are largely guesswork because the only remains that have been found of this animal are some teeth and jaw bones. However, the remains have several interesting features that make it seem likely that* Ramapithecus *was the ancestor of the hominids.*

Sites where fossils of ramapithecines and dryopithecines have been found.

Sites where fossils of ramapithecines and dryopithecines have been found.

The face of an animal that palaeontologists call Sivapithecus, *found in the Siwalik Hills.*

Pakistan that most of the evidence has been found.

David Pilbeam, from Yale University in America, has searched these deposits for several years. He has found that the ramapithecine remains represent animals of three distinct sizes. The smallest is known as *Ramapithecus*; it probably weighed about 20 kilograms (45 pounds). The next, known as *Sivapithecus*, was very similar to *Ramapithecus* but slightly bigger, and the last, called *Gigantopithecus*, was an enormous animal. It was larger than a male gorilla and probably weighed over 272 kilograms (600 pounds). *Ramapithecus* is thought to be our earliest true ancestor, but the evidence is not good enough for us to be completely sure. A species that has not yet been discovered may very well turn out to be the real ancestor of the hominids, that is, modern humans and all the other human-like creatures that once inhabited the earth but are now extinct. For the moment, however, most scientists accept *Ramapithecus* as the earliest hominid.

New places to live

The deposits in the Siwaliks cover a time period of fourteen million to half-a-million years ago, but the ramapithecine fossils have only been found in the earlier layers. After eight million years there are no more ramapithecine fossils. One reason for this may be that between eight million and six million years ago the world climate was again changing. The evidence suggests that there was a drastic cooling of the climate in Pakistan which made it impossible for the ramapithecines to live there.

Unfortunately there is a gap in the fossil record between eight million and four million years ago, but it seems probable that the ramapithecines continued to live in Africa. We know that they lived there before this, since a specimen of *Ramapithecus* that is about fourteen million years old was discovered by my father at Fort Ternan in Kenya, and specimens of *Sivapithecus* are also known from Kenya.

But there are very few deposits of rock in Africa that are between eight million and four million years old. Those that exist are small and widely scattered. Many are located in areas where it is extremely difficult to excavate, so very little work has been done on them. Although we believe that the ramapithecines survived in Africa and evolved into human ancestors there, at the moment there is no evidence to show that this is true.

At the same time as the world's climate was changing, between eight million and six million years ago, major movements of the earth's surface were taking place in the Rift Valley. High mountains and immense, low-lying grassy plains appeared, so that a large variety of new habitats were created. These presented opportunities for new adaptations and evolutionary change. Several of the major groups of plains animals, such as antelopes and horses, made their first appearance at this time, adapting to the new open-country environment.

These movements of the earth's surface in eastern Africa may well have had a very significant influence on the evolution of the ramapithecines at this time. In fact, they may have been the major cause of the split between the apes and humans. The split came when some ramapithecines changed from walking on four legs to walking on two legs.

Two feet instead of four

How did this dramatic change in our posture and gait come about? For many years it was thought that our ancestors began to walk on two legs so that their

A female baboon, carrying its young one, stands on its hindlegs to pick berries from a low bush. Being able to move on two legs is useful when gathering food and this may be why our ancestors first became bipedal. Standing on two legs is also useful for spotting predators, as the photograph on p. 8 shows.

hands were free to do other things such as make tools. But in fact tools do not appear until very much later in our story. Some people now think that the change had more to do with the stomach. When a small animal feeds it can readily stand on two legs to pick fruits, berries and nuts from low branches. I have often seen vervet monkeys standing upright to reach the seeds on long grass, or clusters of berries on bushes. *Ramapithecus* may well have found that, by standing on two legs, it could pick food that would otherwise have been out of reach. And then, by walking on two legs, it may have found that it could carry away handfuls of food to eat quietly on its own, far from the snatching hands of its companions.

There may be a different explanation for the switch to *bipedalism* (walking on two legs), but

however this change occurred it was one of the major milestones in our past. It opened up all sorts of opportunities and led to tool-making, enlarged brains, speech and culture. Unfortunately we do not know exactly when this change occurred, but we do know that by three-and-three-quarter million years ago our ancestors were fully bipedal.

Footprints of the past

In 1976, my mother was working at a site in Tanzania called Laetoli, when a thin layer of rock which had once been a layer of ash was discovered. Ash layers like this are not unusual in East Africa, but what made this layer special was that it had preserved the footprints of birds and animals made three-and-three-quarter million years ago. Most of the prints found in the first year were made by the ancestors of desert hares, guinea fowl, rhinos, giraffes and elephants. But the next year a much more exciting find was made. A colleague of my mother's was out searching for fossil bones when he discovered what looked like human footprints. He showed them to my mother who immediately began work to uncover more of the trail. Several months of excavation followed, during that year and the next, until eventually a trail of footprints nearly 30 metres (100 feet) long lay exposed. The footprints were unmistakably human and, very surprisingly, indistinguishable from footprints made by people today. There were three sets of prints looking very much as if they had been made by two adult humans and a child.

How could my mother be so sure that these were human footprints? The main reason was that the fossil prints show the marks of both the heel and the big toe very clearly. No other animals leave footprints like this: chimpanzees and gorillas have quite different prints.

The fact that there are any prints at all, bird, animal or human, is itself due to a series of lucky chances. Geologists think that the layer containing the footprints was formed when a nearby volcano erupted and a great cloud of volcanic ash showered down. Almost immediately it began to rain, and the ash layer turned to a sticky mud. The animals, birds and humans must have walked across it while it was still wet, but very soon afterwards the sun came out. When the mud dried in the sun it set hard and then a further volcanic eruption covered the prints with a

The oldest footprints in the world – this trail of prints at Laetoli in Tanzania was made almost four million years ago. A large hominid walked along in front, followed by a smaller individual who carefully placed his or her feet in the prints of the first one. This is not an easy thing to do so there must have been some special reason for such behaviour. The third hominid was much smaller, and may have been a child. It walked to the left of the other two, but not alongside either of them – the trails of prints are too close together for this. The footprints show that, even at this early period, hominids could easily walk upright.

second layer of ash. This preserved them for three-and-three-quarter million years, until erosion finally uncovered them.

These footprints are the most dramatic evidence we have that almost four million years ago, there were human-like creatures walking around much as we do today. The creatures who made them are the first that scientists are willing to accept as our undoubted ancestors.

Chapter Four
The man-apes of Africa

The first australopithecines

After the gap in the fossil record between eight million and four million years ago, there are a large number of fossils that can be classified as *hominid* because they are certainly more human than ape. One group of hominids, called the australopithecines, flourished between about four million and one million years ago but then died out.

The earliest australopithecines come from Laetoli, the site where my mother uncovered the trail of human footprints. But the most complete fossil specimens have been found by Don Johanson, Maurice Taieb and Yves Coppens at Hadar in Ethiopia. Hadar is very like the region to the east of Lake Turkana from a fossil-hunter's point of view, covering a vast area and requiring hours of searching over rough country. The fossils are numerous and often well preserved – even crocodile and turtle eggs have survived intact for more than three million years.

One day Don noticed a human-looking arm bone, and then after searching around he found some skull fragments and then more bones. As he found one bone after another he began to realize that he was finding pieces of a single skeleton. For almost three weeks, he and his colleagues combed the hillside looking for more fragments, putting the earth through fine sieves so as not to miss the smaller pieces. Finally, when they put all the fossils together, they found that they had collected almost half the bones of a skeleton. The hip bones were preserved well enough to show that the skeleton had belonged to a female. Such an important find had to have a name, and while

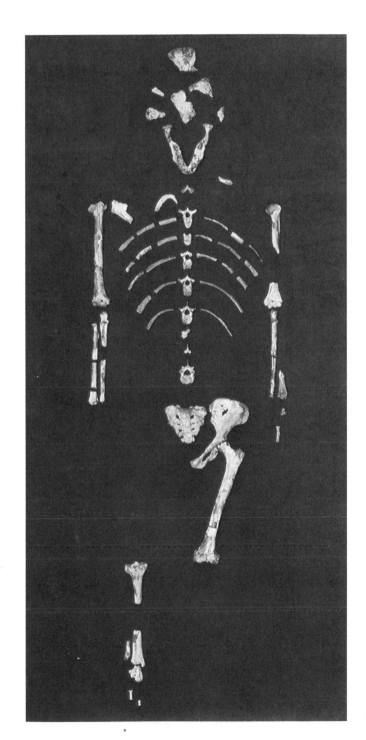

The skeleton known as 'Lucy' is remarkably complete for a find that is over three million years old. The condition of her wisdom teeth reveals that she was about twenty years old when she died, but she already had arthritis in her spine and may have been quite an old lady by the standards of her time.

the fossil-hunters celebrated their good fortune, somebody put the Beatle's song 'Lucy in the Sky with Diamonds' on the tape recorder. They all agreed to call their very special find 'Lucy'.

A fossil called 'Lucy'

Since 1974, when 'Lucy' was found, Don and a fellow scientist, Owen Lovejoy, have been making a careful study of the skeleton. She had a brain between one-quarter and one-third the size of that of a modern person. She was not very tall, only about 100 to 120 centimetres (3 feet 6 inches to 4 feet) in height, and

A reconstruction of 'Lucy', the most complete specimen we have of Australopithecus afarensis. *Although these early hominids walked upright with perfect ease and had hands that are indistinguishable from ours, they did not make stone tools. As far as we know, hominids did not begin to make tools until about two-and-a-half million years ago.*

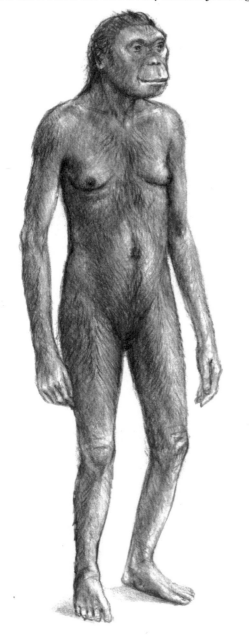

she had long dangling arms. There are no clues to say what caused her death but already she had signs of arthritis in her spine. Don estimated that she was about twenty years old when she died, which was probably quite a long time to live in those days.

To try to find out how human 'Lucy' was, Don Johanson and Owen Lovejoy concentrated their attention on the joints of her leg. They compared the shape of her knee bones with those of modern apes and humans. Unlike apes, the end of a human knee bone is flat. When they looked at the knee bone from the 'Lucy' skeleton it also had a flat end, and from this they deduced that 'Lucy' could, and did, stand upright. Their studies of her hip bones also showed 'Lucy' was much more like a human than an ape. She was probably able to walk and run just like a modern human being.

Both 'Lucy' and the footprints at Laetoli show that more than three million years ago, creatures who stood and walked upright were living in Africa.

Since 'Lucy' was discovered, Don and his colleagues have found many more fossilized remains of our ancestors at Hadar. They believe that all these bones *and* the ones that my mother has found at Laetoli belong to one species which they have named *Australopithecus afarensis*. They think that this species, which lived between four million and three million years ago, was the common ancestor from which all later hominid species evolved. But I and others believe that it may not be quite as simple as this. As I have said, I think it more likely that the common ancestor of all later hominids (species related to us rather than to the apes) lived and died much earlier than this, at the time when our ancestors began to walk on two legs instead of four, probably between eight million and six million years ago. By four million years ago, I believe that the australopithecines and our direct ancestors had already split apart. In my view, 'Lucy' belongs to the australopithecine line.

Later in the fossil record in Africa, the australopithecines become much more common, and they have been found at many sites both in East and South Africa. These fossils are clearly divisible into two basic groups: one is smaller and lighter and is called 'gracile'; the other is much more heavily built and is called 'robust'.

The gracile australopithecines

The gracile type, whose scientific name is *Australopithecus africanus,* was first discovered at a limestone quarry called Taung, in South Africa. Here, in

1924, the quarry manager discovered a child's skull. He knew enough about bones to know that the skull was probably important, and he sent it straight away to Raymond Dart, a fossil expert at the University Medical School in Johannesburg. It arrived with a lot of other rocks in a big dusty chest just as he was about to set off for a wedding. He was so excited that he nearly missed the ceremony and ruined his best suit into the bargain.

The next day he took the chest into the laboratory and looked more carefully at the skull. Although the brain was small and ape-like, the rounded skull and the shape of the teeth made Dart think that it belonged to a remote human ancestor: he called his discovery a 'man-ape'.

In 1924, nothing like this skull was known and Dart's 'human ancestor' was met with disbelief; he had to wait nearly twelve years for more evidence. This was provided by a retired doctor called Robert Broom. He was world famous for his work on fossil reptiles, but he was so excited by the discovery of the Taung skull that he gave up everything else to concentrate on trying to find more fossils like it. Broom looked at cave after cave without success until eventually he found the remains of a similar skull at a cave in South Africa called Sterkfontein. This skull belonged to an adult but it was obviously

of the same species as the Taung child. Soon more fossils were found and at last scientists began to take them seriously.

More recently we have found similar specimens in East Africa. The most complete have come from Olduvai Gorge and the region to the east of Lake Turkana. The East African skulls are even more lightly built than the South African ones, but they probably looked very much alike as living creatures.

They must have been about 120 centimetres (4 feet) tall, and, to judge from their leg and hip bones, they

A reconstruction of the gracile australopithecines, small hominids who inhabited wooded areas of Africa between two-and-a-half million and one million years ago. The male and female did not differ much in size.

The skull of a gracile australopithecine found at Taung. The skull had a full set of milk teeth but the first adult teeth were just emerging – this means that the Taung child was less than six years old when it died.

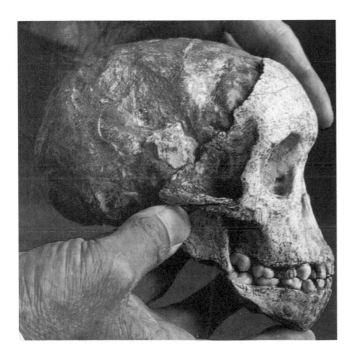

were capable of standing upright and walking and running on two legs. Their brains were not much larger than those of gorillas, but their bodies were much smaller. This means that the gracile australopithecines were probably a little more intelligent than gorillas or chimpanzees.

The robust australopithecines

The robust type, called *Australopithecus robustus*, was much bigger than the gracile type and had massive jaws with huge flat molar teeth. The South African fossils have come mainly from two caves called Swartkrans and Kromdraai, while the best specimens from East Africa have come from Olduvai Gorge and the region to the east of Lake Turkana.

The first of those to be found in East Africa was discovered by my mother in 1959. My father had remained in camp feeling unwell while my mother set out with her two Dalmatian dogs to search for fossils on her own. Looking carefully at a promising cluster of bones she noticed two teeth which were unmistakably of the hominid type. She rushed back to camp to tell my father who of course immediately forgot his illness and hurried with her back to the spot.

Over the next few months an enormous excavation took place which unearthed the greater part of a skull broken into over 400 fragments. My mother fitted the fragments back together until she eventually had an almost complete skull. This skull was even bigger and more strongly built than those of the South African robust australopithecines, but it was certainly similar. Its molar teeth were three or four times the size of ours, and there was a large bony ridge on the top of the head where the massive chewing muscles would have been attached. This skull was nicknamed 'Nutcracker Man' by the newspapers.

Australopithecus rides a camel

Apart from this skull, the only other fossils of robust australopithecines from East Africa were a couple of teeth and a piece of thigh bone from Olduvai, and a jaw from Peninj in Tanzania. But in 1969, I discovered another complete skull near Lake Turkana. It was only my second expedition to this enormous area and we were still exploring. At that time, it seemed the best way to explore was on camel. On this occasion we had stopped early the previous day because the camels needed time to graze. Rather than move on early we decided to spend the next morning searching the sediments close by our camp. Kamoya and his companion, Nzube, went off in one direction, while

Two skulls of robust australopithecines. On the right is the skull found at Olduvai Gorge by my mother, Mary Leakey, in 1959. This is the skull which earned the name 'Nutcracker Man'. On the left is the skull which I found near Lake Turkana almost exactly ten years later.

Meave and I went off in another. It was a very hot morning and we found few bones. By about ten o'clock we decided to go back to the camels to have a drink and a rest.

Feeling discouraged by our lack of luck we were ambling down a dry sandy riverbed when I suddenly saw the unmistakable shape of an australopithecine skull lying on the sand ahead. There, unbelievably, was a complete skull of a robust australopithecine. It had fallen out of the bank of the now dry riverbed in the last heavy rain some weeks before. If we had not discovered it then the next rain would probably have swept it away, smashing it to smithereens against a rock.

When Kamoya and Nzube eventually arrived, they were as amazed as we were. Together we carefully removed the loose sand from around the skull and then placed it in a biscuit tin lined with sheepskin from one of the camel blankets. Then we loaded our camels and turned back the way we had come, taking our treasure safely back to camp. It was certainly the first australopithecine to ride a camel!

In the following years, Kamoya and his team of helpers have discovered many specimens of the robust australopithecines near Lake Turkana. From these specimens and a number from other sites we now have a good idea what this type of early hominid looked like. A large male would have weighed about half as much again as a gracile australopithecine. It would have been about 150 centimetres (5 feet) tall,

A reconstruction of the robust australopithecines, who lived in Africa at the same time as the gracile australopithecines, but inhabited more open country.

The skull of a robust australopithecine male (right) *and a female* (left). *The male was much more heavily built and had enormous jaws and teeth. The muscles which operated this massive chewing apparatus were attached to a bony crest on the top of the skull.*

but very heavily built, like a gorilla. Its broad flat face, strong jaws and large teeth were better suited for chewing large quantities of tough food.

If you hold your fingers against your cheeks and try clenching and unclenching your teeth, you will feel the muscles moving which operate your jaw. Strong muscles would have been needed to move the huge jaws of the robust australopithecines, and on their skulls there are bony ridges to which the muscles were fixed. Whatever food they ate, they certainly had to work hard at their eating. The females were much smaller than the males and they did not have such large muscles or big bony ridges.

The silence of the caves

One problem with the australopithecine fossils which Dart and Broom found in South Africa is that it is impossible to tell exactly how old the limestone caves are. There are no volcanic rocks rich in potassium, nor does limestone contain any chemicals which can be dated. A rough estimate of the age of the caves can be made by comparing the bones of animals found in the caves with those from other sites that can be dated chemically, but this does not always give a very precise date.

In East Africa where the sediments are laid down one on top of another, and sandwiched between layers of volcanic rocks, good dates can be obtained. Here both species are found in fossil sites between about three million and one million years old, so it looks as if the gracile and robust australopithecines lived at the same time. However, the two species may have been living in different kinds of country. Elizabeth Vrba, Deputy Director of the Transvaal Museum, decided to find out if this was so in South Africa. She looked at the fossil antelope bones found in the caves with the gracile and robust australopithecines. First she looked at the bones from Sterkfontein where the gracile australopithecines had been found, and here she found that there were only a few plains antelope with the *Australopithecus africanus* remains. But in two other caves where *Australopithecus robustus* had been found there were many bones of plains antelope. Studies of the fossil pollen in the caves also showed that the vegetation where the robust australopithecines lived was largely grass. So it seems that in South Africa the gracile australopithecines preferred more wooded areas to live, while the robust australopithecines preferred the grassy plains, which is why their fossil remains are not found together in the same caves.

How did they die?

Some of the South African caves have an enormous number of fossil bones in them. More than a quarter-of-a-million fossil animal bones have come from one cave alone. How did so many bones become buried in one place?

For a long time it was thought that it was the work of leopards that took their prey up into the large trees which often grow at cave entrances, and dropped bones into the mouth of the cave. But when Bob Brain, the Director of the Transvaal Museum, looked more closely at the bone collections he found that there were many more baboons, monkeys and australopithecines than any other animal. He wondered why this should be so and one evening he decided to find out. Just as it was getting dark, he went into a large cave near his home, hid himself and waited. After a while, a troop of about thirty baboons

Excavations at Swartkrans cave in South Africa. The rock found inside these caves is known as breccia and was formed from soil, rocks, bones, and other debris falling into the cave. There is no chemical method for dating these deposits, so it is difficult to say exactly how old the South African australopithecines are.

A robust australopithecine from Swartkrans – marks on its skull show how it died, for they fit exactly with the teeth of a leopard skull found in the same cave.

entered the cave and began to settle for the night on a rock ledge. Bob waited and then when all was quiet he showed himself. The animals panicked, jumping and leaping everywhere, but they would not leave the cave to escape into the dark night. Bob thinks that the fossilized baboons, monkeys and australopithecines found in the caves may have been caught in this way. They would have made easy prey for an agile carnivore such as a leopard, lion or sabre-tooth cat.

Who were the australopithecines?

So who were these hominids? They were obviously successful as they lived a long time. They were not very clever, judging by their rather small brains, so they probably could not have made stone tools. The males were much taller and more heavily built than the females, particularly among the robust australopithecines. These robust types were probably eating tough, unnourishing food because they had very specialized teeth with huge surfaces for chewing. Both species could walk and run around and they probably climbed trees. They were clearly more human-like than ape-like, but on the whole they do not seem to have had the characteristics we would expect of our true ancestors.

Chapter Five

The earliest people

The tool-maker

In 1960, my elder brother, Jonathan, found a jaw of a young child which was clearly not a robust australopithecine. This was followed by other finds: leg bones, hand bones and a foot. All were much less rugged looking than the robust australopithecines. The specimens did not have the strong skull ridges or massive teeth and they also had a larger brain.

The first thing that my parents had to decide was whether these bones belonged to a gracile australopithecine. They compared them with the specimens from South Africa since at that time *Australopithecus africanus* had not been found in East Africa. It looked as if the Olduvai fossils were a slightly different shape and, in particular, they had a much bigger brain. This larger brain persuaded my parents that the hominid that Jonathan had found would have been clever enough to make tools. They were convinced that here was a different sort of early hominid from the australopithecines, and they put it into the special group to which modern man belongs, *Homo*. They called it *Homo habilis* which means 'skilful man'.

What was just as important about these finds was their age. Some of them came from the same rock layer as 'Nutcracker Man'. This proved to my parents that the robust australopithecines were not our real ancestors. They were more like our cousins, living alongside the true human family for two million years or so before becoming extinct.

'Skilful man' from Lake Turkana

As you might imagine, some scientists were not at all convinced that *Homo habilis* was anything more than a gracile australopithecine. They argued the case

A reconstruction of the hominids known as Homo habilis *who lived about two million years ago. We can be reasonably sure that these people were our direct ancestors and the first to make stone tools.*

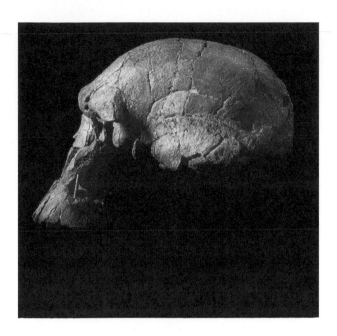

In 1972 an extremely important skull was found near Lake Turkana by Bernard Ngeneo, one of my fossil-hunting team. Known as 'Skull 1470' this is the best specimen we have of Homo habilis. *It had been broken into hundreds of pieces, which were carefully joined together again, the smallest fragments being matched under a microscope.*

back and forth, but all they could agree on was that they needed more evidence. This came not from Olduvai, but from the region to the east of Lake Turkana where, in 1972, one of Kamoya's team, Bernard Ngeneo, found a two-million-year-old skull, known by its museum number '1470'.

Bernard's sharp eyes spotted a few fragments of the skull on the slopes of a small hill. He immediately recognized them as human and with careful searching up and down the slope he found more pieces. When we examined the pieces back in camp they looked very insignificant, but since they were coming out of the sediment at the top of the hill, I hoped that by sieving all the sand and gravel on the slope beneath we might find more.

We were lucky. Gradually each day, as the hot, dusty work of sieving continued, we found more and more fragments. Meave had the job of fitting them all together. She would anxiously wait for me to return each day with more of the fossil jigsaw puzzle until, after about three weeks, we had an almost complete skull, although the face was still incomplete. I was impatient to know the size of the brain, since I could see that it was a lot bigger than the brain of a gracile or a robust australopithecine. The normal way to estimate the size of the brain is to fill the skull with sand and then pour the sand into a measuring cylinder half-filled with water and measure the displacement of the water. We had plenty of sand in camp, but no measuring cylinder. Then someone had the bright idea that we could use the rain gauge. This we did and we found that we had the equivalent of 20 centimetres (8 inches) of rain. This was a brain volume of about 800 cubic centimetres, almost twice as much as the 450–550 cubic centimetres of the australopithecines. This was surely the tool-maker, *Homo habilis.*

There were still many tiny fragments to put together, mostly from the face. After three weeks, Meave decided that she needed the help of our friend Alan Walker, so we took the skull back to Nairobi, where together they finished the jigsaw. '1470' was one of the most complete of the fossil skulls and provided all sorts of new information about *Homo habilis.* Later that year and in following years we found more specimens of jaws and other bones. These all showed us that while *Homo habilis* had a differently shaped skull to modern humans, the bones of his body looked very similar. The skull was different from ours because it had a smaller brain case, a longer face and stronger jaws with larger teeth.

The first tools

While fossil bones and teeth can tell us a certain amount about what our ancestors looked like, how they moved and what sort of food they ate, bones and teeth say very little about behaviour. Although we grumble today about people who leave bottles and cans behind after a picnic, archaeologists rely very much on the fact that our ancestors were just as bad as we are at tidying up before they moved on. Their litter is what archaeologists work on.

Part of the litter our ancestors left behind consisted of stone tools. The earliest tools we have found are simple stone flakes about two-and-a-half million years old from two sites in Ethiopia: the Omo Valley and Hadar. The discovery of how to make a stone flake was a major breakthrough in our evolution. If a round hammer stone is knocked against another suitable rock, sharp flakes are chipped off which can be used to cut up animals. Scavenging meat from kills using only hands and teeth is almost impossible if the animal is at all large. But with sharp flakes, it is possible to skin an animal, remove the meat from the bones and cut the meat into small pieces. Flakes can even cut into the tough hide of elephants and hippos. The simple flake must have made it possible to eat all sorts of new foods.

Reconstructing the landscape

When we find these early tool sites, what do we learn from them? At one time archaeologists thought that only the stone tools could tell us about the way of life of the people. Now they are beginning to realize that the sorts of places where the tools were left also have a meaning. Did the people wander all over the place, just stopping when they were tired or had found food? Or did they choose their camp-sites more carefully, looking for clean drinking water, shade and protection from wild animals?

Geologists can tell us what the landscape was like. They can locate lakes, rivers, streams and valleys and put together a detailed picture of the ancient countryside. Using these reconstructions the archaeologists can plot where the sites were located. In this way we can find out whether our ancestors preferred to camp by the lakeshore, on the shady banks of a river or out on the open plains.

A stone flake can slice through thick hide (even elephant hide) and can be used to cut joints of meat from a carcass. This enabled our ancestors to scavenge meat from large animals that had been killed by predators or had died naturally, thus increasing the food available to them.

If you could be transported back two million years into the past this is what you might see at Olduvai Gorge. Instead of dry, dusty rock there was a lake where crocodiles, hippos, pelicans and flamingoes lived. Along the lakeshore small bands of hominids set up camp.

Olduvai Gorge

As we have seen, the best fossils of *Homo habilis* have come from Olduvai Gorge and the region to the east of Lake Turkana. So too has the best evidence of the behaviour of *Homo habilis*. Two million years ago there was a large lake where the Gorge at Olduvai is now. Like many African lakes, this one was not full of fresh water, but was rather salty. Fresh water ran into it from streams on its eastern side, but no river

left it. In years when it rained heavily, and the days were cool and cloudy, the lake level rose, while in years when the sun blazed down and the sky was clear, water evaporated and the lake became shallow and even more salty. In spite of this, fossils show that the lake was always full of fish such as catfish and tilapia. It was also the home of at least one very large species of hippopotamus and two sorts of crocodile, one of which had a big, broad snout and powerful jaws. The lakeshore also teemed with life, and more fossil birds have been found at Olduvai than at any other two-million-year-old site. Ducks, pelicans, flamingoes, cormorants and grebes all nested in the reeds and paddled in the lakeside pools. Even in the dry years, the climate was wetter than it is now. A good guide to how moist the ground must have been are the remains of fossil slugs and the bones of shrews that only live in damp grass.

The lake was surrounded by open woodland, and taller trees grew along the banks of nearby streams and rivers. The types of mammals living then were much the same as today, though to judge from their bones, most were bigger than their modern relatives. We know that elephants and giraffes browsed on the leaves of the trees, and that gazelle, rhinos, antelopes and pigs were feeding out in the open. There were also a few strange animals which are now extinct, such as a big sabre-tooth cat and a giant deinothere, a curious elephant-like creature with tusks that curved downwards.

Life beside the lake

Two million years ago at Olduvai, our ancestors seemed to prefer making their camps along the eastern end of the lake, where the streams and rivers flowed in. Altogether my mother has discovered eighteen sites there. Despite years of searching, only two possible sites have been found over on the western shore of this ancient lake.

The sites are of two sorts. There are the places where our ancestors actually made camp, and other places where they simply stopped for a while to cut up an animal carcass. Most of the camp-sites were situated by the water's edge, and at one of the biggest there are the fossil remains of papyrus reed which shows that it was swampy.

The animal bones found at the camp-sites look as if they were broken deliberately; on some of them you can even see cut marks made by stone tools cutting away the meat. Antelope meat seems to have been their favourite food, with three-toed horses and zebras a close second. The bones of fish and turtles also suggest that they were making good use of the lake itself. When other sorts of food were scarce it looks as though our ancestors were not above eating small birds and even chameleons.

The first huts

My mother has made very detailed plans of all the ancient camp-sites, and at two of these she thinks that the people may have built some kind of shelter. At one the signs are that there was a sort of wind-break; at another, she thinks they may have even managed to build a proper hut. Here she found a series of quite large stones arranged in a circle. As the inside of the hut would have been used for sleeping most of the tools and broken bones were scattered over the ground outside the circle. A circle of stones does not seem much evidence of a hut, but even to this day people living in the arid, windy areas of northern Kenya support the struts of their grass huts with stones. When the hut burns down, or the wood is eaten away by termites, all that remains is a circle of stones just like the one at Olduvai.

Three of the sites that my mother examined look more like the remains of a primitive butcher's shop than a camp. At each one there are the remains of a single animal: an elephant, a deinothere and a giant buffalo. Apart from the broken bones of these animals, the only other signs of human activity are the tools. My mother thinks that these animals were driven towards swampy ground. Once in the swamp,

the animals would soon have become exhausted with their efforts to save themselves from sinking, and would have then been easy prey for their pursuers. The carcasses would have been far too big to drag out of the sticky mud so the best solution was to butcher them on the spot. The smaller pieces of meat could then be easily carried back to a camp nearby.

The people of Lake Turkana

We now move 1,000 kilometres northwards to the east shore of Lake Turkana. Here, two million years ago, the lake was larger than it is today and as at Olduvai the climate was wetter. The fossil pollen shows that there was even a thick forest not too far away. Glynn Isaac has been searching here for evidence of sites where early hominids lived. The first one was found in 1969, and since then Glynn and his colleagues have been studying large numbers of sites every year.

The first thing they noticed was an obvious similarity with the sites at Olduvai: some of the sites near Lake Turkana were camps, while others were places where animal carcasses were cut up. Unlike Olduvai, however, the Lake Turkana sites were not right on the edge of the lake, but on the banks of streams flowing into it. Another difference was that at Olduvai the sites were often occupied for long periods of time so that thousands of tools and bones were mixed up together in a small area. At Lake Turkana the sites had been occupied for very short periods so there were far fewer tools and bones and it was much easier to work out what the people might have been doing.

One of the Lake Turkana butchery sites was on the sandy bed of a stream on a small delta. A group of our ancestors had apparently come across a hippopotamus stranded in a pool not far from the lake. There are no signs of how it was killed; it may have been dead already. But whatever happened they set about the task of making stone tools to cut up the carcass. There were no pebbles nearby so they must have brought suitable stones from far away; either they made a special journey to fetch them or they were carrying them around anyway. Whatever the case, they left behind a number of flakes, several cores from which the flakes had been struck, and a round hammer stone.

The site that has provided Glynn with the most information about our ancestor's way of life is known as Karari Site 50. Here, one-and-a-half million years ago, our ancestors were camping on the bank of a river which at least in places held water. Here 1,500

A seasonal stream near Lake Turkana. It was beside a stream such as this that a small group of hominids camped for a few days, one-and-a-half million years ago. The litter they left behind them is today being uncovered by archaeologists at Site 50. It was probably buried quite quickly by sediments as the waters of the stream rose, just as this oryx skeleton is being buried. Because the litter was buried rapidly but gently it was not greatly disturbed, and archaeologists now see the remains of camp very much as it must have looked when the hominids left. Overleaf is a reconstruction of the Site 50 camp-site based on the evidence found.

stone fragments and 2,000 bone fragments have been recovered by an excavation which took nine months to complete. The site was apparently occupied for a relatively short period of time which made it simpler to interpret much of the evidence. Luckily the site

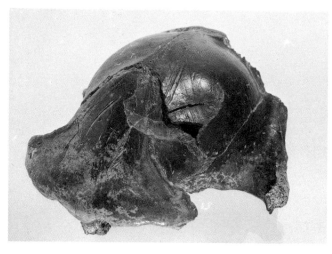

The skull of a baboon found at Olduvai Gorge. Small cut marks can be seen in the bone, presumably made by the stone tools of our ancestors who killed these monkeys for food. Similar cut marks are seen on some of the bones found at Site 50, confirming that the hominids who camped here were using stone tools to butcher animals.

Another bowl of sand and stones removed from the Site 50 excavation is taken away for sieving. This is done to recover small fragments of bone and chipped stone that may contain vital clues about what went on at the site. During a nine-month excavation no less than 1,500 stone fragments and 2,000 bone fragments were recovered.

was buried gently by the floodwaters of the river, so it was preserved much as the hominids had left it when they moved on.

Broken bones and stones

One of Glynn's students, Nick Toth, taught himself to become an expert stone knapper. He learned to understand the techniques used by our ancestors and to produce identical tools. At Site 50 they found sixty cores; Nick can tell that the flakes had been knocked off these cores in the same way, using a rather unusual technique. He says that to produce all the flakes and cores found at this site would be no more than an hour's work for one person.

Another student has studied the bone fragments; he has identified the remains of a number of animals including two species of hippo, zebra, pig, giraffe, an eland-sized antelope and a catfish. By studying the larger fragments he has found that some of the long bones were broken by smashing them with a hard object. This was probably to enable the people to get at the marrow. There are also cut marks on some of the bones made by stone flakes as they were used to cut away the meat.

Windows on the past

These scenes from our past are like little windows that we can peep through to glimpse a scene here and a scene there. Unfortunately some of the windows are shut so we can never see the whole picture. At first glance the broken animal bones of butchered carcasses at all these sites suggest that our ancestors were determined hunters who ate nothing but lots of meat and a little fish, but this could be entirely wrong. Plant foods were probably eaten in large quantities as well, but these leave no trace in the fossil record.

Glynn believes these scenes indicate one very important change in behaviour: our ancestors were sharing food with other members of the group. The variety of animals apparently eaten at one spot suggests that these hominids carried their food back to a camp-site to share with others. If the carcass was too large it was cut up on the spot and smaller pieces carried back as in the case of the hippo. Plant foods were probably gathered and brought back to camp as well although we have no fossils to show this.

Today there are a few people who still pursue a somewhat similar way of life: they are called hunter-gatherers. By talking to such people we can learn a little bit more about a way of life that must be quite similar to that of our ancestors.

Carrying all their possessions, and their smallest children, a band of !Kung people move on to look for a new camp-site. Like other hunter-gatherers, they do this whenever the local food supply runs low. The litter they leave behind in the abandoned camp-site looks remarkably like that of ancient camp-sites such as Site 50.

The life of the !Kung

The !Kung San live in the Kalahari desert in the general area of Namibia and Botswana. (The !Kung language includes many clicking sounds which are represented in writing by '!K' and other symbols.) Although the Kalahari is called a desert, there are actually a lot of trees, bushes and grasses in this incredibly flat country. Until very recently, most of the !Kung used to live in temporary camps, in groups of about thirty people. The women would gather plant foods and look after the children, while the men hunted wild animals. When the food close to camp became scarce, they would move on to another area. This kind of life is probably as close to that of the early hominids as we can get in the modern world.

Anthropologists have studied the remains of !Kung camp-sites and kept careful records of camp life, including what food the people ate and how the food was obtained. When the !Kung abandoned a camp-site the anthropologists found that the litter left behind, the animal bones and broken tools, looked very similar to the litter found at the ancient camps at Olduvai and Lake Turkana.

The !Kung people taught archaeologists an important lesson. They now realize that the things they find in the ancient camps are only those that have managed to survive for nearly two million years. Digging sticks and animal-skin containers are as important to the !Kung as stone tools, but because they are made of wood and skins they do not last. That is why the litter from archaeological sites suggesting that our ancestors were only meat eaters, is so misleading. Like the !Kung, they probably relied mainly on plant foods.

A new way of life

It is likely that our ancestors also hunted and gathered, collecting food and bringing it back to a home base to be shared. It is unlikely that this could have been achieved unless our ancestors had some sort of language. Archaeologists believe that our ancestors succeeded where the australopithecines failed because they were the first to break through into a new co-operative way of life which could adapt to and exploit new circumstances. Simple as human life was two million years ago, it was the beginning of a completely new pattern of evolution. Physical characteristics were changing but our ancestors were becoming more intelligent. Cleverness depends on what people do, not what they look like. So you will find that from two million years ago onwards, we take more and more notice of what our ancestors were doing, and pay rather less attention to the shapes of their bones and teeth.

Chapter Six

The big-game hunter

The australopithecines disappear

Between one-and-a-half million and one million years ago, East Africa seems to have experienced a major change in climate. The lakes got smaller, rivers dried up, and forests and woodlands were replaced by more open grassland or savanna. As before, this change provided opportunities for evolutionary change. New animals appear in the fossil record and others die out. Of course, this change affected our ancestors too. During this time, we first find remains of an ancestor with a larger brain and a more sophisticated toolkit than that of *Homo habilis*. It is towards the end of this period that the australopithecines become extinct and instead of three hominids living at the same time, there remains only one.

Although the first fossils of *Homo erectus* were found over eighty years ago in Java and China, it was not until 1960 that this species was found in East Africa. In that year my father found a very large skull with strong brow-ridges at Olduvai Gorge: *Homo erectus* probably lived there about one million years ago. This find established the presence of *Homo erectus* in Africa, but it did not explain how it came to be there. Did *Homo habilis* evolve directly into *Homo erectus* or did *Homo erectus* evolve from some other ancestor? Perhaps *Homo erectus* evolved in Indonesia or China and then moved back into Africa. At present we do not have enough evidence to say for certain, but I believe that *Homo erectus* first appeared in Africa.

The earliest Homo erectus

In 1975 Bernard Ngeneo made a discovery in the region to the east of Lake Turkana which filled the gap between the one-million-year-old *Homo erectus* skull from Olduvai and the 1.8 million-year-old *Homo habilis*. Bernard spotted the brow-ridges of a human skull just protruding above the surface of the soil, and then found fragments of the face scattered nearby. When I saw the skull, I realized that it would

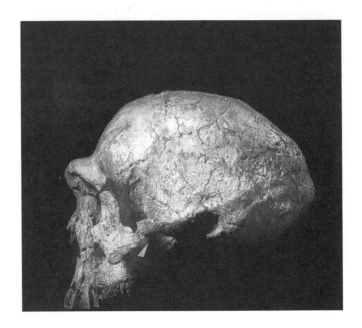

The Homo erectus *skull found by Bernard Ngeneo in 1975. The most noticeable features of* Homo erectus *were the heavy brow-ridges and the fairly large brain case.*

need great care to extract; I could see the fine fibres of grass roots extending into the bone. These roots cause immense damage: as they penetrate the fossil they produce acid which causes the bone to turn to powder. The work was so delicate that it took me two days, slowly taking off the surrounding soil a millimetre at a time with a small dental pick and a fine paint brush. As each fraction of the bone was exposed, I put a drop of hardening substance onto it. At last the skull was ready to remove. I was delighted as this was the earliest evidence of *Homo erectus* anywhere in the world. It was almost half-a-million years older than the only other East African specimen from Olduvai, and probably a million years older than the examples from China.

When we took the specimen back to Nairobi, Alan Walker had the difficult task of fitting together the tiny fragments of the face. He had to match some of the smallest pieces under a microscope, but he gradually managed to piece together the nose bones, the cheek bones and finally the upper jaws and teeth. We now had the most complete specimen of *Homo erectus* ever to have been found.

The only way in

But then Alan had another problem. The skull had been found lying upside down, and must have been buried in that position. Sand had filled the brain case and it had gradually turned into sandstone: it was rock hard and very heavy. Alan wanted to see inside the skull, and to do this we had to find a way of removing this very hard rock without damaging the skull itself. The hole at the base of the skull was too small to allow Alan to remove the rock with the usual dentist's drill. We therefore decided to crack the fossil skull in half. Taking a hammer and chisel, Alan made a few tentative blows, but nothing happened. He got a larger, harder chisel and gave a hard quick blow that split the skull along existing cracks into two pieces. Alan could then drill the rock away so that we could look at the marks left on the inside of the skull by the brain – marks that can tell us something about brain structure.

The usual way to remove rock from fossilized bone is with a dentist's drill. Here a drill is being used to clean up the skull of a robust australopithecine.

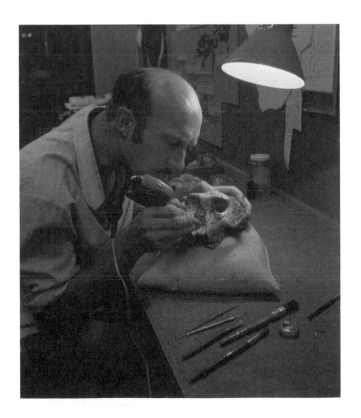

So many fossils of Homo erectus *have been found that we have a fairly good idea of what these hominids were like. Their bodies were short and stocky but not all that different from those of modern humans. However, their heads looked very different. Heavy brow-ridges jutted out above the eyes, the forehead sloped backwards, and they had rather ape-like muzzles. The mask worn by this actor shows what* Homo erectus *looked like when alive. We can be certain that he had dark skin to withstand the glare of the African sun.*

Putting flesh on the bones

The brains of the new skulls were between 900 and 1,000 cubic centimetres in volume which was larger than those of the earlier *Homo habilis*. Other differences were that the smooth, backward-sloping forehead of *Homo habilis* had been replaced by a big bony brow-ridge jutting out over the eyes. The *Homo erectus* skulls were also flatter on top and extended further backwards. Instead of curving evenly down towards the neck, the backs of the new skulls were angled more sharply inwards. Their faces had a more human profile.

One thing that we can be fairly sure about is that the skin of the first *Homo erectus* people living in Africa was dark in colour. Dark coloration is needed by people living in the tropics to prevent the strong sun from damaging their skin. Our more distant ancestors may have had lighter skin because, like all other primates, they would have had a thick covering of body hair which protected them from the sun. But at some time in our past we developed a highly efficient body cooling system: sweating. Human beings sweat more readily and profusely than any other living animal.

For sweat to cool the body effectively, it must be able to evaporate quickly and thick body hair would stop this happening. Our ancestors therefore developed the covering of hair that we have today, where there are lots of hairs but most are very fine. As this happened they must have developed darker skins too and it is likely that both *Homo habilis* and African *Homo erectus* had this extra pigmentation.

A typical Homo erectus *handaxe. The first step in making such a tool was to strike a large flake. Then the edges of the flake were carefully chipped away until they were sharp and the tool came to a point at one end. The rounded end was probably gripped in the palm of the hand when the axe was being used.*

However as *Homo erectus* moved out of Africa and further north, the pigment in the skin had to become reduced. This is because the human body needs vitamin D, and vitamin D is produced in the skin when it is exposed to sunlight. In tropical regions where the sun is strong, it can penetrate even the most pigmented skins. But in more northerly regions where the sun is weak, heavy pigmentation prevents the formation of vitamin D. So we can assume there would have been a tendency for the skin colour to lighten as our ancestors moved northwards.

Evolving skills

At about the same time as *Homo erectus* first appears in the fossil record, there is also evidence for more sophisticated tools. As well as the simple flakes typical of *Homo habilis*, more complex variations of the flake appear which look as if they have been designed for chopping, piercing, cutting and pounding. The most common tools were the handaxe and the cleaver. These are like extra-large flakes: to make them you strike a big flake from a very big core. The cleaver, which is basically a flake with a sharp straight edge, then only requires a little trimming, but the handaxe which is pointed and may have a cutting edge all round is often a work of art.

The tools we find are remarkably standardized and remain basically unchanged from one-and-a-half million years ago until 200,000 years ago: this phase of the Stone Age is named the Acheulean.

Homo erectus: big-game hunter at Olduvai?

Although animal bones found at the earlier sites suggest that *Homo habilis* was butchering animals and taking meat back to camp, there is no real proof that these people were hunting rather than just scavenging from carcasses or taking the occasional opportunity to capture a sick or unwary animal. Various later sites suggest that *Homo erectus* was a true hunter and much better organized for co-operative hunting.

At one Olduvai site, my mother found the remains of twenty-four rather fierce-looking buffalo-like creatures with long pointed horns. They were found in what the geologists think was once a swamp, or a quiet backwater of a river. One skeleton was found buried in an upright position, as if the buffalo had become stranded in the mud. Choppers and a make-shift handaxe were found close by, and it may be that the early hunters had driven the herd into the swamps and killed and butchered them there. At a second site there are signs that a herd of small antelope may have met a similar fate.

Another clue that makes us suspect that *Homo erectus* was a hunter comes from a series of round stone tools which archaeologists call spheroids. Some of them are naturally smooth, others show the marks where they were chipped into shape. They may have been used as missiles to bring down game. Some South American hunting tribes still use such a weapon, known as a bolas. It consists of three stone spheres, wrapped in leather bags, and joined together by long leather thongs. Grasping the thongs at the point where they meet, the hunter swings the spheres round his head, and then lets them go so that they fly towards the prey. The bolas wraps itself around the animal's legs, bringing it to the ground.

Hunting giant baboons

At Olorgesailie in Kenya, there is further evidence of *Homo erectus* hunting. Today the area is hot and dry, but about 600,000 years ago the water of a lake attracted all sorts of animals. Here our ancestors left an amazing number of beautifully made handaxes, concentrated at several small sites. At one of

these sites, the remains of more than sixty giant baboons were found. The baboons were mainly juveniles and young adults, suggesting that *Homo erectus* had selected those of a certain age and did not catch the very large adults or small babies. The adult males of this species of baboon reached an impressive size, not much smaller than a female gorilla, so they must have been quite a formidable prey.

As a teenager, I started up a business supplying small animals to research laboratories and spent many months capturing baboons. I devised several methods of doing this, but two were particularly effective. Baboons generally prefer to stay close to the large trees found near rivers and streams, but now and again I would find a troop out in the open, feeding on the grass while crossing between two

At the site of Olorgesailie in Kenya the remains of over sixty giant baboons have been found, together with thousands of handaxes. Groups of Homo erectus *hunted these formidable animals here over half-a-million years ago. A walkway has now been built so that visitors can look at the site without damaging the remains.*

rivers. On these occasions, I could stalk up to the troop, getting quite close without being seen; then I would run into their midst. They would immediately take off with me running among them. I was relatively fit and I found that I could actually run faster than the baboons. As I ran, I would select my animal and grab it, and the rest of the troop would run on, leaving me with my captive.

Another less exhausting method of catching baboons was to frighten a troop in a tree at dawn before the animals woke up. While it was still dark, I and one or two companions would approach the

Actors wearing Homo erectus *masks re-enact a scene that must have occurred millions of times during the course of human evolution, whenever small groups of our ancestors sat down in the shade to share the plant foods they had collected – nuts, berries, leaves and roots – as well as meat obtained by hunting or scavenging.*

tree in which the baboons were sleeping. I would stop under the tree while my companions would walk on, fooling the baboons into thinking that we had all departed. Then as it became just light enough to see, my companions would come back and the baboons would immediately start jumping out of the tree. Because they were all half-asleep and it was still too dark to see properly, they often landed very badly. For one or two seconds on landing, individuals would be stunned, which gave me just enough time to catch one. If I had had a club, I could easily have killed a number of them. No doubt *Homo erectus* would have been much fitter than I was and could have devised equally successful methods for catching the larger, more intimidating baboons at Olorgesailie.

A surfeit of liver

All these clues – more elaborate tools, butchered animal herds and stone missiles – strongly suggest that *Homo erectus* was a successful hunter and meat-eater. But yet another different sort of clue has come from a skeleton found in the region to the east of Lake Turkana.

Several years ago, parts of a female *Homo erectus* skull and skeleton were found on a hillside at a site not far from our camp. The hill was covered with fossil bones of all sorts of animals, but one feature of this hominid skeleton made it very distinctive. It was diseased. Over the surface of all the bones a second layer of bone of varying thickness had been deposited making it easy to pick out from the other bones. Because of this we were able to recognize even the smallest fragments of the skeleton until eventually we had the most complete skeleton of *Homo erectus* ever found.

We were interested to know what disease had caused this. Alan Walker showed it to some doctors who recognized it as a disease of the bones, caused by an overdose of vitamin A. Although today the disease is rare, one way of getting it is to eat too much raw liver. Maybe this individual *Homo erectus* gorged herself on the liver of a large animal with fatal results.

Chapter Seven

The people go north

The long trek to China

Only when our ancestors became so skilful at hunting that they could rely on meat as a source of food, could they risk moving out into new, less predictable climates. Just before a million years ago, there are signs that *Homo erectus* was beginning to move northwards out of Africa. By studying a series of camp and fossil sites we can follow their movements.

First they travelled northwards through Africa. Butchery sites about a million years old in the highlands of Ethiopia, show that our ancestors were then hunting large animals such as hippos. By this time *Homo erectus* clearly knew how to keep well fed in a wide variety of environments.

Other sites have been found in Israel and Syria. Apart from the usual food remains and stone tools,

This map shows the major sites where remains of Homo erectus *have been found. The oldest remains, dating back one-and-a-half million years, are found in East Africa, but about a million years ago these hominids began to move northwards and by about 70,000 years ago remains turn up in Europe, China and Java.*

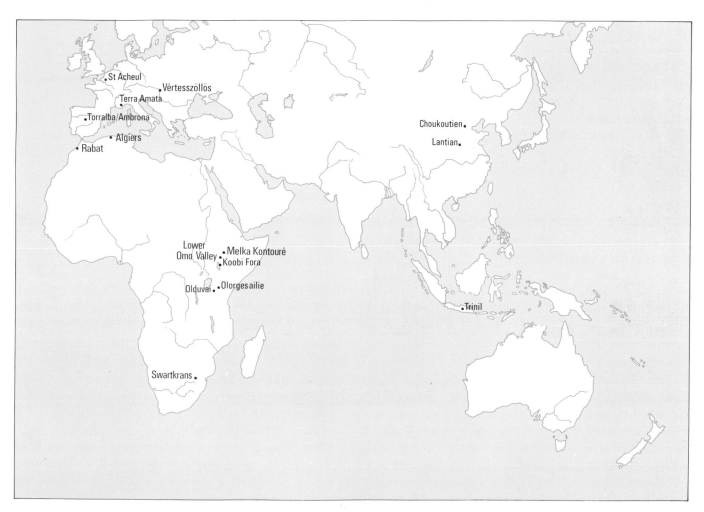

the Syrian site includes piles of rubble which may be the remains of the base of a shelter. The variety of hunted animals now becomes very impressive: elephants, rhinos, bison, horses and even camels.

Not long after this, but certainly less than 700,000 years ago, fossils of *Homo erectus* are known from several sites in Europe, and similar fossils have been found in China and Java. If we are correct about the age of the Java fossils, then it took nearly half-a-million years for *Homo erectus* to reach the Far East.

The hunt for Java Man

For many years *Homo erectus* was known as Java Man because it was there that the first distinctive skulls were found in 1891. The discovery was made by a Dutchman called Eugene Dubois. Although he had been trained as a doctor he had always been fascinated by strange animals and fossils. He used to make a point of going to listen to every possible lecture about evolution and the origin of mankind. A lecture by a German zoologist, Ernst Haeckel, and a book by a British biologist, Alfred Russel Wallace, convinced Dubois that the East Indies, the home of the orang-utan, might be a good place to find fossils of our ancestors. He joined the Dutch army as a doctor, and was sent to the Dutch colonies of Sumatra and Java, now part of Indonesia.

Dubois first spent time in Sumatra, but to his great disappointment the fossils he found were only a few thousand years old. Two years later, he was posted to Java, and things began to look more promising. He heard that fossils had been seen along the banks of the Solo River. It was the dry season when he arrived and the water level was very low, exposing parts of the dry riverbed. In one of the exposed areas he caught sight of the top of a human-like skull sticking out of the mud. The face and base of the skull were missing, but a tooth was found nearby. More than a year later a thigh bone turned up at the same place. It was this thigh bone which originally gave *Homo erectus* its name. It looked so like the bone from a modern human thigh that Dubois knew that its owner must have walked upright as we do: *erectus* means 'upright'.

Dubois was convinced that his skull and thigh bone belonged to the long-sought-after 'missing link' between modern humans and apes. Today we know that there is no such 'link' between modern humans and modern apes but in the nineteenth century those that believed in human evolution thought that a direct link would be found. They were also convinced that it would be found in Europe and few of the

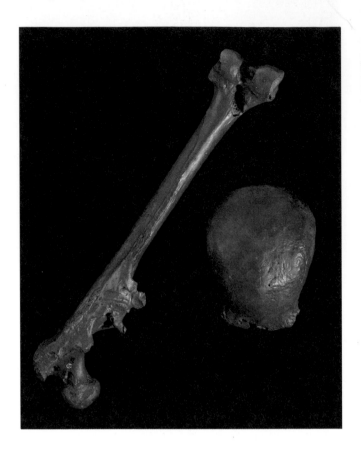

The Homo erectus *skullcap and thigh bone found by Dubois in Java at the end of the last century. The thigh bone clearly showed that its owner had walked upright.*

experts would take Dubois's finds seriously. Towards the end of his life he became so depressed that he took to hiding his precious fossils beneath the floorboards in his bedroom!

Dragon Bone Hill

The story of how *Homo erectus* came to be found in China starts in a chemist's shop. This was no ordinary chemist's shop, however, but a store selling traditional herbal remedies. The Chinese place great faith in the healing powers of fossils, which they call 'dragon bones'. In 1903 a German professor was looking through a drawer full of medicinal fossil teeth when he came across one that looked rather human. He asked the owner of the shop where the tooth had come from, and eventually traced it back to some caves near Peking. But it was not until 1926, in a cave on a hill called Dragon Bone Hill, near the town of Choukoutien, that any more human teeth were found. The cave was large and literally full of bones. Two teeth were just the first of many human fossils to be found: there were skulls, jaws and arm and leg bones.

(Above) *An entrance to the cave in Dragon Bone Hill, near Choukoutien, where Peking Man lived half-a-million years ago. The cave was first excavated in 1926 by Professor Davidson Black, a Canadian working at the Peking Union Medical College.*

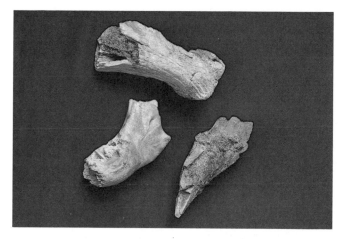

(Right) *Bones from the Peking Man cave show signs of having been burned – this is the earliest evidence of our ancestors using fire. Deep layers of ash inside the cave suggest that fires were kept burning constantly, perhaps to scare off animals as well as for warmth.*

Some of the tools found in the Peking Man cave – these include the handaxes typical of Homo erectus *together with cruder tools for chopping, pounding and breaking bones, and small sharp tools made of quartz that may have been used for skinning animals.*

Unlike the South African caves, there was clear evidence at Choukoutien that the people had made these caves their homes. The camps had obviously been lived in for some time and judging from the huge piles of ash, *Homo erectus* had kept fires burning almost continuously. The cave dwellers were obviously efficient hunters and had a particular taste for deer because there were more deer bones in the caves than any other animal. There were typical handaxes found in the cave, and many small, sharp tools made of quartz.

The mystery of the Choukoutien fossils

Incredible as it may seem, no one knows where the fossils from Choukoutien are today. During the Second World War, the fossils were believed to be at risk and so they were carefully packed up in crates and put on a train to go to the port of Chinwangtao. There a ship was waiting to take them to the United States for safe keeping. But the fossils never arrived. Somewhere on the train journey or in the port they were lost. From time to time, people claim to know where these valuable fossils are, but so far it has always proved a false trail and they are still missing. Fortunately a set of excellent casts had been made of the fossils before they were lost, and new excavations at Choukoutien have resulted in more finds.

A Mediterranean camp-site

Although relatively few *Homo erectus* fossils have been found in Europe and North Africa, there are several sites where tools and litter have been found around the Mediterranean, and as far north as Hungary and Germany. In recent years a few fossils of the hominids themselves have also been found. The fossils add little to what we know already of *Homo erectus* from Asia and Africa, but three sites, Terra Amata in France and Torralba and Ambrona in Spain tell us something of the life of these early European people.

The site at Terra Amata came to light in 1965 when foundations were being dug for a block of flats in Nice. Though the site now lies on the corner of a busy street, less than half-a-million years ago it was ideally placed on a sheltered, sandy beach at the point where a small river flowed into the Mediterranean Sea.

A reconstruction of the hut built at Terra Amata. Tree branches were pushed into the sand and supported around the outside by blocks of stone. The hominids then meshed the branches together, over a central row of sturdy posts, to form an arch, and probably laid foliage over this structure to keep out the wind.

Here archaeologists have found the remains of eleven huts that had been built on roughly the same spot year after year. The huts were oval in shape, about 12 metres (40 feet) long by 6 metres (20 feet) wide. The walls were probably made of young branches, supported in the middle by a row of sturdy posts – the holes made by these were still clearly visible almost half-a-million years later.

Near the centre of each hut a hearth was found, and scattered stone flakes showed that the people had made tools inside the hut. The shells of limpets, oysters and mussels were found as well as the bones of a great variety of animals that the people had eaten – red deer, elephant, wild boar, mountain goat and even a rhinoceros.

The area was clearly only inhabited for a short period, and always in the late spring, to judge from the fossil pollen found. The hut collapsed soon after the band departed (although on one occasion it seems to have been burned down) and the autumn winds then covered the whole area with a thick layer of sand, thus preserving the evidence for us to find.

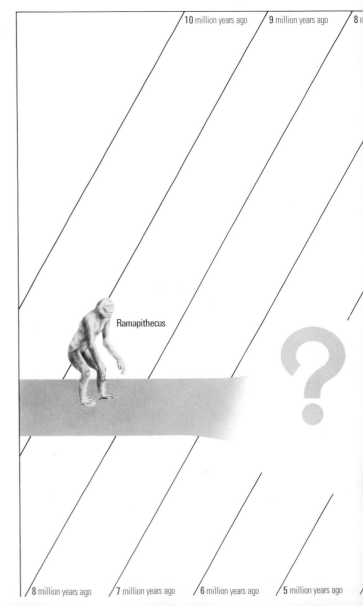

Ramapithecus

Hunting elephants in Spain

From excavations at the sites of Torralba and Ambrona, it seems that other *Homo erectus* hunters were making regular visits to this Spanish valley to hunt large numbers of elephants, horses, red deer, fallow deer and wild oxen. There is evidence at some places that single animals were trapped, their legs removed and what remained of their bodies cut up and taken back to camp.

The hunted animals were too many and each too large to be handled by just a small group of hunters. At one place, it is estimated that nearly 20 tonnes of

This diagram shows the various hominid species that have been found and when each one lived. The grey horizontal lines indicate the most likely relationships between these hominids and the question mark is placed over the fossil void, a crucial period in our evolutionary history, but one for which we have almost no evidence. As can be seen, Homo erectus was followed by two forms of Homo sapiens, Neandertal Man and fully modern man. The story of Neandertal Man is taken up in the next chapter.

meat were carried away from kills which included three elephants, two red deer and a wild ox! This suggests that the hunters were in well organized bands of perhaps twenty or thirty people – maybe more. The stone tools used to butcher these carcasses are much better made than the early African stone tools and there are signs that the tools were being resharpened when they became blunt.

The dawn of human life

The contrast between the simple camp-sites of *Homo habilis* and the organized hunting, sophisticated huts, fires and hearths of *Homo erectus* is a dramatic one. The handaxes used by these later people were often works of art, and tools were always made to the same pattern. There is also evidence of coloured pigments, such as red ochre, at some of the sites which suggests that *Homo erectus* was beginning to think of things other than where the next meal was coming from. Perhaps the colours caught the imagination of the hunters; maybe they painted it on their bodies or on to stones.

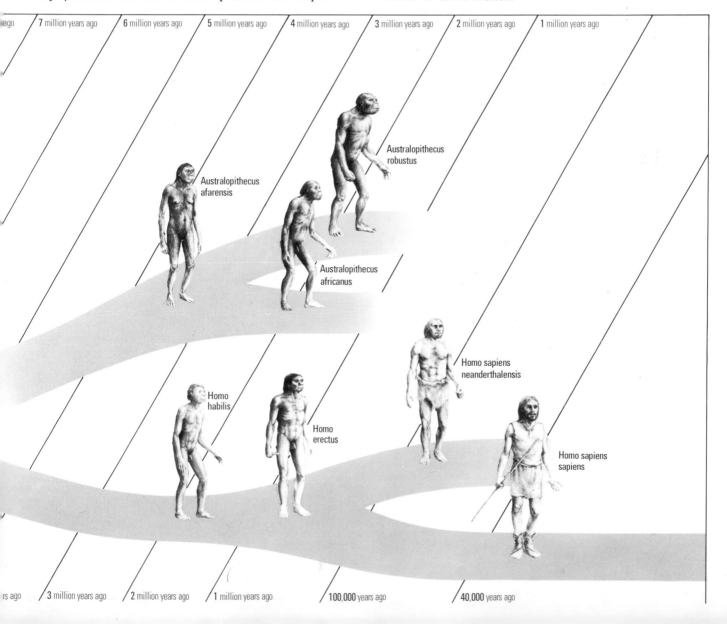

7 million years ago | 6 million years ago | 5 million years ago | 4 million years ago | 3 million years ago | 2 million years ago | 1 million years ago

Australopithecus afarensis

Australopithecus africanus

Australopithecus robustus

Homo habilis

Homo erectus

Homo sapiens neanderthalensis

Homo sapiens sapiens

3 million years ago | 2 million years ago | 1 million years ago | 100,000 years ago | 40,000 years ago

The hunting, the tools, the huts and the possible use of ochre, all suggest that human society had become much more complicated during the past million years. *Homo erectus* was no longer just a tropical hunter-gatherer, but a successful, well equipped species who had learned to cope with the chilly climate and the changing seasons of the northern latitudes. In the next chapter we will see how these early populations of *Homo erectus* are related to the type of people that replaced them.

People in various parts of the world still use natural pigments like red ochre to paint their bodies – two different South American tribes who practise body-painting are shown here. Decorating the body in this way is usually part of some religious ceremony or special ritual, or an indication of tribe membership. Pieces of ochre, sharpened into points as if used for drawing, have been found in several Homo erectus *sites suggesting that these hominids may have begun to think about things other than where their next meal was coming from.*

Chapter Eight

Neandertal Man

A species in transition

How did the change from *Homo erectus* to *Homo sapiens* come about and where? We know that *Homo erectus* was a relatively stable species between one-and-a-half million and half-a-million years ago, and then between 400,000 and 200,000 years ago, we begin to find skulls showing a mixture of *Homo erectus* characters and *Homo sapiens* characters. These skulls are found in Europe, Asia and Africa. So did *Homo sapiens* evolve in one place and then spread through the rest of the world? Or did our species evolve simultaneously in Africa, Asia and Europe? We do not yet know exactly what happened.

One of the most complete skulls showing this mixture of characters from Europe was found in a limestone cave near the village of Petralona in Greece. The finder of the skull is now a very old man: his name is Christos Sarianniddis, but the villagers of Petralona call him Uncle Philipos. While herding his flocks on the hills he had noticed a crack in the ground from which cool air came even on the hottest summer day. Thinking that it might lead to a source of water, which would be useful to the village, he took four friends to investigate. They climbed down into the cave but, finding no water, they quickly left. A year or so later, however, the men went back to the cave to have another look at some strange skulls they had seen down there. This time they discovered a hominid skull, covered with a layer of white crystals, stuck to the wall of the cave. Uncle Philipos took it to the Thessaloniki University where it was recognized as a link between *Homo erectus* and *Homo sapiens*. It had the brow-ridges, low forehead and large face of *Homo erectus,* but the larger brain of *Homo sapiens*. Another similar skull was found in a gravel pit in the village of Swanscombe near London. And yet another skull of similar age came from Steinheim in West Germany. This skull also had a mixture of characters – prominent brow-ridges, a gently sloping forehead, but a well rounded brain case.

This skull, found in a limestone cave near the village of Petralona in Greece, shows a strange mixture of characteristics. Some, like the prominent brow-ridges, are reminiscent of Homo erectus, *but others, particularly the large brain case, are more like* Homo sapiens.

In a cave in the foothills of the French Pyrenees, known as the Arago cave, fossil bones of an enormous variety of animals have been found: rhino, elephant, musk ox, cave bear, giant sheep, lion, panther and beaver. There were also the remains of thousands of rodents in the cave. Among all these bones, Henri de Lumley and his wife Marie-Antoinette, have found part of a skull which seems to be a late *Homo erectus*

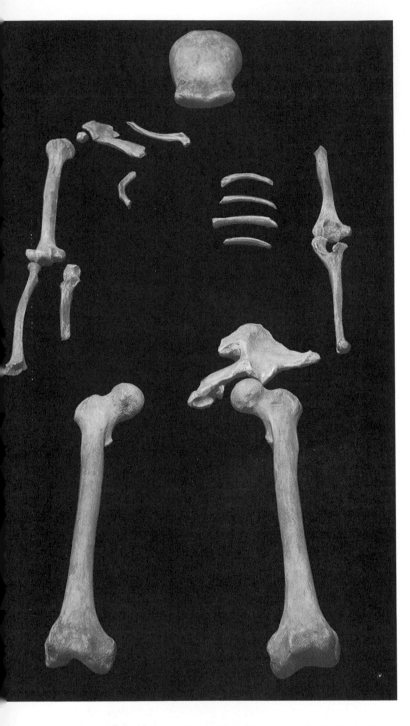

This male skeleton, found in a little cave in the Neander Valley in 1856, caused an uproar. To the people of the nineteenth century Neandertal Man seemed a highly unsuitable candidate for the ancestor of the human race. Almost everyone tried to disown him in one way or another – some dismissed him as an ape, while others tried to attribute his physical characteristics to disease. The most popular explanation was that he was a Cossack (hence the short, sturdy frame) suffering from the disease known as rickets, which had bowed the bones of his legs. It was also suggested that the pain he endured from rickets made him constantly furrow his brows, producing prominent bony brow-ridges above the eyes!

or early *Homo sapiens*. The most interesting thing about this cave was that instead of the sort of hand-axes which had been found at earlier *Homo erectus* sites, there were more skilfully made choppers and lots of small, delicate tools which showed signs of having been sharpened and resharpened. It seems as if these people who had changed physically from earlier *Homo erectus* had also made advances in their tool-making skills.

There are many skulls which have been found that show this mixture of characters and it seems likely that there was a gradual change from *Homo erectus* to *Homo sapiens* which began about 400,000 years ago. By 100,000 years ago we find skulls which are fully *Homo sapiens*. There are, however, still many evolutionary steps between the earliest *Homo sapiens* and modern humans like ourselves.

Neandertals – our Ice Age cousins

Early *Homo sapiens* appears at roughly the same time in Africa and Asia, but we know most about this period of our past in Europe. This is because European archaeologists have been busy looking for remains of prehistoric people for over a hundred years, whereas elsewhere the search did not begin until quite recently.

The early *Homo sapiens* of Europe that lived between 100,000 and 40,000 years ago are called Neandertals. The Neandertals take their name from the Neander Tal, which literally means 'the valley of the Neander'. The Neander is a small river which runs into the river Dussel, not far from the modern city of Dusseldorf in West Germany. In 1856, quarry workers were clearing out the bottom of a cave when they uncovered part of a skull and some limb bones. They collected all the bones and took them along to the local doctor for his opinion. He realized at once that they were human and sent them on to the Medical School in Bonn where they were examined by the Anatomy Professor, Dr Schaafhausen. After looking at them carefully, he came to the conclusion that they were indeed the bones of some kind of human being.

A Cossack with rickets?

The shape of the skull caused consternation among many scientists. No one wanted to believe that it had belonged to a human ancestor. It was long and low, with little or no forehead, and some experts of the day even thought it might have belonged to an ape. Others thought that the skull was human and that the odd shape was due to the effects of disease. The most popular view was that the skeleton belonged to a Cossack soldier who had died while retreating from the Napoleonic wars and who had suffered from a bone disease called rickets. A British scientist, Charles Lyell, re-examined the cave to check the workmen's story and returned convinced that the fossils were truly ancient. Thomas Huxley, an English biologist, was the first to notice that even though the skull was flat on top and lacked a modern type of forehead, it nonetheless had a brain as big as that of modern humans. Because of this he thought that the skull was likely to have come from a man, but one who was more primitive than ourselves.

Because the discoveries from the Neander Valley virtually coincided with the publication of Charles Darwin's *The Origin of Species*, the remains excited wide interest. As it turned out, the Neandertal fossils were not the first remains of this kind to be found. A child's skull had been found earlier in Belgium, and an adult skull had been discovered in Gibraltar as early as 1848, but nobody had realized their importance at the time.

As the years went by similar looking, but better preserved, skulls were unearthed in Belgium, France and Yugoslavia. These made it more and more difficult for people to maintain that the original Neander Valley finds were an oddity produced by disease although it was clear that the Neandertals were a distinct group of people who were not quite as advanced as modern humans.

Shaking off the 'ugly brute' image

If we take a look at the Neandertal skeleton, it is undoubtedly human, although there are several minor ways in which it differs from our own. For a long time some of the differences, such as the large joints and the big, rather bowed limb bones, led scientists to think they were primitive. The first reasonably complete skeleton was found in France in 1908, and by chance it happened to be from an old person who had arthritis. When the experts of the day examined the skeleton they did not realize it was diseased, and when they saw the bent neck and stiff-looking joints they were convinced that Neandertals were very primitive indeed. Their conclusion was that the Neandertals could not walk properly, but only shuffled along with their heads bent forwards, their backs stooped and their long arms hanging down by their sides.

Now that many more Neandertal bones have been found which are not diseased, scientists have very

The idea that Neandertal Man was round-shouldered, shuffling and dim-witted was a popular one, as this old reconstruction shows. But it was entirely wrong – the skeleton on which this was based had belonged to an old arthritic man – healthy Neandertals looked and walked very much like ourselves.

different ideas about what these people looked like. It has become clear that they could walk just as well as we do and were equally good with their hands. Their leg bones *were* bowed, and the joints *were* big, but this is just because they were much more muscular than we are. Marks on the bones of the shoulder suggest that they had particularly powerful arms. But in spite of this they did not differ that much from modern humans. In fact if we were able to dress a Neandertal man and woman in modern clothes, cut their hair and put them into a modern airport, they would probably go unnoticed by the other passengers.

A profile of the Neandertals

Although Neandertal skulls are long from front to back and flat on top like those of *Homo erectus*, they are very much bigger. In fact, the average brain size of the Neandertals was actually larger than that of

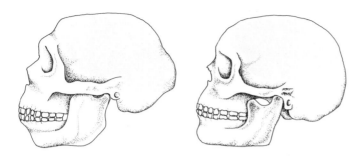

Although the Neandertal head (left) *was differently shaped from ours, with a low, sloping forehead, the brain was actually slightly larger than that of modern man.*

humans today. The skulls have characteristic bulges at the sides and back; the French called the one at the back a 'chignon' because it reminded them of a woman's hair done up in a bun.

Another feature of the Neandertal skulls is the shape of the face. Instead of being flat the nose and the jaws stick forward, so that the cheek bones slope backwards. This means that the teeth are set much further forward than they are in modern man, and consequently there is no obvious chin.

Their strange projecting faces and muscular limbs have led some people to believe that the Neandertals were especially suited to withstand the cold. Research has shown that a muzzle-like face is ideally

In the Ukraine great piles of animal bones have been uncovered, the remains of shelters built by Ice Age hunters. The reconstruction on the left is of a Neandertal shelter, 44,000 years old. Animal skins were stretched over a wooden frame and weighted down with mammoth bones. The shelter could have accommodated over thirty people and several fires burned inside for warmth. On the right is shown a much later hut, 13,000 years old, built on the same site.

shaped to cut down the chances of frostbite. Their stocky bodies – they were on average about 1.67 metres (5 feet 8 inches) tall – would have cut down heat loss like those of present-day Eskimos. But this does not explain why Neandertals with these characteristic features were also found in the Near East where frostbite was never a problem, so perhaps there is another explanation.

The Neandertal landscape

Nearly all Neandertal fossils are found at sites which are between 100,000 and 40,000 years old. Most of them are in France, Belgium and Italy but there is a trail of sites leading right across Europe, from the Atlantic coast of Portugal in the west, to the Russian steppes in the east. The Neandertals must also have ventured south because their remains are found at a few sites in the Near East.

Neandertals first appear in the fossil record when the world was relatively warm. This was between 130,000 and 75,000 years ago when there was a warm period between two cold spells of the Ice Ages. But the last Ice Age began about 70,000 years ago, so during most of their existence the Neandertals were experiencing one of the coldest spells the world has ever known. It was during this time that the Neandertal characters became fully developed. They lived in conditions that people had never experienced before and they survived them by being inventive and resourceful. In the very cold regions there was little grass and few trees, so they burned bones in their fires and made huts by stretching animal skins over a framework of mammoth bones and tusks. Fortunately there were numerous animals such as reindeer, mammoths and cave bears to provide them with plenty of meat. When available, caves provided shelter and we know that the Neandertals devoted

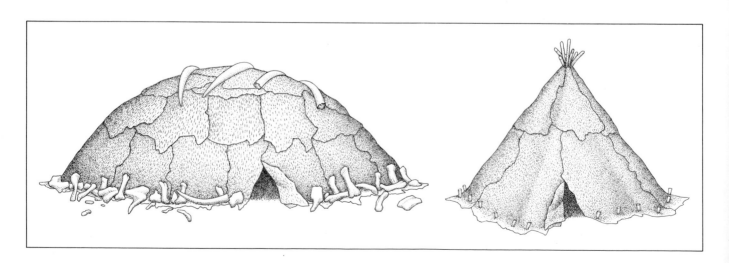

much time, energy and skill to preparing animal skins. With warm clothes and fire they made the best of the cold weather.

Remains found at many Neandertal sites suggest that they did not stay in one place for very long. Instead they moved from camp to camp in their search for food. Sometimes the food remains suggest that the Neandertals ate a varied diet, but more often it seems that they concentrated on hunting one particular sort of animal. At one site nearly all the bones are from young cave bears, whereas at another they all come from baby mammoths. In general, however, their staple diet seems to have been wild horse and reindeer meat.

Specialized tools

Neandertals are associated with a much more diverse toolkit than that of the earlier *Homo erectus*. A greater variety of tools were prepared from one flake and over sixty different tools have been recognized. These tools were also prepared much more skilfully and precisely than anything that had been made previously.

The Neandertals hunted with spears and bolasses (see p. 45). Just as they tended to concentrate on hunting particular kinds of animals, they also made much more specialized tools. Instead of making them from whatever rock happened to be nearby they nearly always used flint. Flint is not found everywhere so if there was no local source a Neandertal tool-maker presumably travelled to the nearest flint area to collect some. The tool-maker may have bartered skins or meat with someone who could supply this special raw material. We know of one 40,000 year-old flint mine in Switzerland, where the Neandertals battered lumps of flint from seams that are visible in the limestone rock.

Neandertal customs

There are signs in the way they buried their dead that the Neandertals recognized a spiritual aspect to life. At Le Moustier in France, a teenage boy was buried lying on his side with his head resting on his arms. A pile of flints lay under his head and a beautiful stone axe lay near his hand. All around him were the bones of wild cattle. It is easy to imagine that these things were put in his grave to help him on his way after his death. At another site called Teshik Tash in Central Asia, a young child was buried with six pairs of ibex horns arranged in a ring around his head. And at Shanidar in Iraq, where many remains of Neandertal Man have been found, one man had a very special burial 60,000 years ago. Dense clusters of fossil pollen show that flowers were arranged around the body making a colourful grave of white, yellow and blue. The flowers are all medicinal herbs suggesting the possibility that the man was some sort of doctor and these were the herbs he used in his medicines.

Other burials show that the Neandertals looked after the elderly and the sick. Many of the people buried were well advanced into old age, and one skeleton was of a man who was clearly very badly crippled during his life.

The Neandertals lived in Europe when the weather was at its worst and we would not expect there to have been very many of them. But in fact more Neandertal skeletons have been found than skeletons of all their European ancestors put together. One reason for this is that the Neandertals seem to have been the first people to make a point of burying their dead. Before this, the discovery of our ancestor's bones depended on a series of chance events, but when people bury their dead there is a greater chance that the skeletons will be preserved as fossils.

The Neandertal puzzle

The fossils and tools of the Neandertals disappear quite suddenly from the European fossil record about 35,000 years ago, and they are replaced by those of the more modern-looking 'Cro-Magnon' people.

While Neandertals were living in Europe, other modern-looking humans were living in Africa. One of the best known of these is Rhodesian Man from Broken Hill in Zambia. But there are other finds too, from Saldanha in South Africa, from Ngaloba in Tanzania and from Bodo and the Omo Valley in Ethiopia. Skulls and limb bones from these African sites show that by at least 100,000 years ago, people were even more modern-looking in Africa than in Europe. These people did not have the stocky, rugged characteristics of the Neandertals. This is possibly because they were not adapted to the extreme cold.

At one time it was thought that the Neandertals were replaced by more modern-looking people from elsewhere, who took them over by force and slaughtered them all. But there is no evidence of any such massacre or bloodshed and the truth is probably

(Overleaf) *A reconstruction of the scene at Shanidar when Neandertals buried an old man, surrounding his body with flowers. In other Neandertal burials the bodies were sometimes surrounded by stone tools or animal bones.*

57

a lot less dramatic. There is now good evidence that the Neandertals themselves evolved into recognizably modern people. Some of the later skulls show a mixture of Neandertal and modern features, and at some tool sites we can actually trace the change from typical Neandertal tools to the more finely made flint blades and spear points of their Cro-Magnon successors.

But it does look as if the process of this evolution was speeded up by the arrival of more modern-looking people from elsewhere. It is probable that these people integrated peacefully with the Neandertals by intermarrying, and the Neandertals may have acquired more skilful techniques of tool-making from them. Once they had learned the delicate tricks of making long flint blades, fine knives and spear points, the need for a big strong body and powerful arms was much less. As big bodies also need proportionately more food to keep going, natural selection would have tipped the balance in favour of skilful, but more lightly built people.

The caves of Mount Carmel

Three sites are known in Israel that date from the time of this transition, and which should help to solve the problem. In the cave of Tabun, on the slopes of Mount Carmel, two individuals have been found that are 45,000 years old and show Neandertal characters. A few hundred metres away in the cave

Some of the sites at which early forms of Homo sapiens *have been found. The finds from Petralona, Arago, Swanscombe and Steinheim show features intermediate between* Homo erectus *and* Homo sapiens. *True Neandertal fossils are found only in Europe and Asia; the early* Homo sapiens *people of Africa looked more modern.*

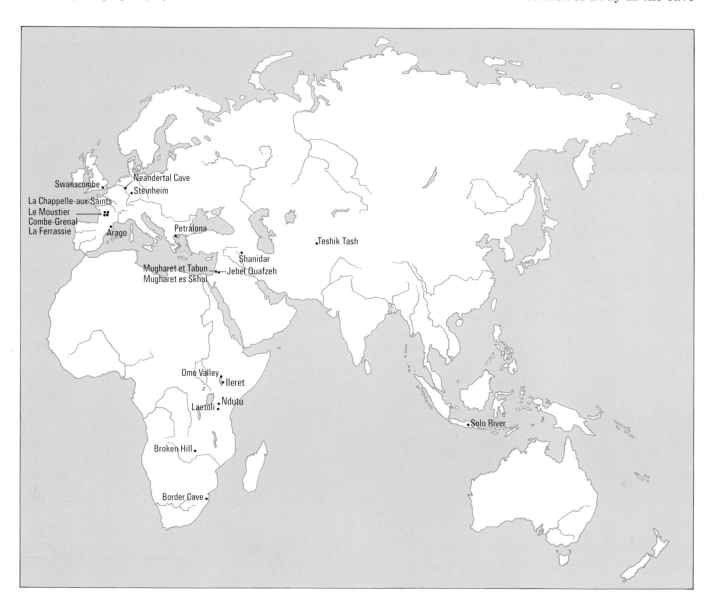

of Skhul, the skeletons of ten individuals who are probably 40,000 years old show more modern features. At the third site, Jebel Qafzeh, eleven skeletons similar to those at Skhul have been found, but the tools found with them are generally typical of the Neandertals.

The simplest way to explain these skeletons is to say that the Tabun individuals represent the earlier Neandertal population which later intermarried with a more modern immigrant population, and that the Skhul and Jebel Qafzeh people are the result of this intermarriage. Unfortunately anatomists tend to differ in their interpretation of these skeletons and the explanation may not be as straightforward as this.

The discovery of new lands

There are no signs at all of people getting to America and Australia until just over 30,000 years ago, by which time fully modern people were well established all over the rest of the world. The reason for this is quite simple: America and Australia were cut off from elsewhere by the oceans. But during the coldest part of the Ice Age much of the water from the earth's oceans froze into glaciers and ice fields. This caused the sea level to fall and the area of submerged land which joins northern Asia to North America was exposed. This enabled people to cross on foot into the New World. The fall in sea level also exposed a string of islands between Southeast Asia and Australia, so that Australia could be reached by a series of short voyages, probably made in simple canoes.

Fishing canoes made from a single, hollowed-out log, set sail from the Caroline Islands in the Pacific Ocean. It was in simple canoes such as these that the ancestors of the Aborigines reached Australia about 30,000 years ago. The earth was then in the grip of an Ice Age, and because so much water was 'locked up' as ice in the glaciers and the polar ice-caps, the sea level fell. This exposed many small islands so that the voyage from Southeast Asia to Australia became a series of short journeys from one island to the next. New Zealand was colonized many thousands of years later by people from Polynesia.

Ideas, not bodies, now evolve

To all intents and purposes the physical evolution of humans all over the world was complete by about 20,000 years ago. We do not see any further major changes in the skulls, teeth and skeletons of human beings. But what now begins to evolve very rapidly are ideas, skills and ways of living.

By 20,000 years ago, people had a rich culture. The walls of caves are decorated with paintings; stones and bones are carved and engraved. Finely made needles and pins suggest that much more care was being taken over clothes and shoes, and jewelry seems to have been worn. Food too was becoming more varied and interesting; fishing was well organized with carefully made hooks and harpoons. People seem to have had some form of religion, a sophisticated language and what we would think of as a social life. In fact life with these people of the last 20,000 years would not seem all that strange to a visitor from the twentieth century.

Chapter Nine

The first artists

Mysterious caverns

One of the most dramatic experiences of my life was to visit Le Tuc d'Audoubert, a cave in the Dordogne region of France owned by Count Robert Bégouën. To get into this cave you have to first travel by boat and then clamber for several hours through very narrow passages into the depths of the hillside. Count Bégouën kindly offered to show me this spectacular cave which few people have had the privilege to see since it was discovered in 1912.

The cave is very long and throughout its length thousands of beautiful, sparkling white stalactites hang from the roof. Large white stalagmites have grown up from the floor in extraordinary shapes to meet them. As we went into the cave we sometimes had to crawl on hands and knees and in one place we literally had to lie on our stomachs and heave ourselves up a narrow shaft by pulling with our outstretched arms and pushing with our feet. Every now and then we saw the skulls of cave bears lying on the rocks as they had been left about 15,000 years before. The front teeth of all of them had been removed to make necklaces or lucky pendants. One of these necklaces had actually been left behind. As we went deeper and deeper into the earth, I realized how easy it would be to take a wrong turn and get hopelessly lost. But here and there, the leg bones of cave bears had been arranged to point the way.

It was a strange sensation going so far into the hillside and knowing that nothing had been disturbed since our ancestors had departed so many thousands of years before. Here and there were footprints looking as fresh as if they had been made yesterday; some were even made by children. Why had these people come so far into the earth? We found it very difficult to clamber through some of the passages, even though we had torches; how much more difficult it must have been with only flickering animal-fat lamps to light the way, and no matches to relight them if they went out!

At the end of the cave, the passage widens into a small, low chamber and in the centre are two beautiful clay bison, each about 75 centimetres (30 inches) long. They are standing one behind the other and they seem extraordinarily alive. Not far from the bison is a smaller chamber in which the clay floor is covered by a thin layer of calcite crystals. Under the calcite is a hollow which is roughly the shape and size of one of the bison; it must have been here that one of the bison was originally sculpted. Five rolled-up sausages of clay which may have been intended to be used to model details, lie nearby, and the tip of a stalactite which may have been used to dig the partially sculpted bison out of the clay floor. Most surprising of all, the floor of this chamber is covered with the heel marks of human feet, but there is not *one* impression of a toe. The people who made the bison must have walked around this chamber in a very peculiar fashion. These caverns were obviously used for some sort of magic or religious ritual, but what exactly took place in the caves will always remain a mystery.

Underground art galleries

In the Dordogne region of France and in the Pyrenees, there are many other long, branching cave systems. Paintings and engravings of Stone Age artists have been found in many, but the most spectacular are found at two caves known as Lascaux and Altamira.

(Top) *The bison found in the cave known as Le Tuc d'Audoubert. The bison were probably sculpted in the clay that formed the floor of the cave and then prised out by means of a stalactite. The people who made the bison walked about in the cave on their heels so that their toes left no imprint in the clay. Why they made the difficult and dangerous journey into this cave to mould these bison will always remain a mystery.*

(Bottom) *A painted stag from the cave of Lascaux, France.*

At Lascaux, in southwest France, the walls and ceilings of a series of caverns are covered with leaping, jumping and fighting animals, all boldly drawn and looking incredibly lifelike. Paintings of bulls, horses and stags predominate: many are running or charging, some are quietly grazing, a few have been wounded by arrows. One group of deer are shown swimming a river. The artists depicted horses' manes flying in the wind, stags with their antlers poised in challenge and animals gripped in their death throes after a hunt. They added many other animals, including ibex, bison, lions, a bear and even a rhinoceros. The action and movement which these artists of 14,000 years ago managed to capture is truly astounding.

At Altamira, near the northern coast of Spain, similar scenes have been painted on the ceiling of a cave. Almost two dozen bison are painted in red and black on the ceiling of a low chamber with two horses, a wolf, three bears and three deer on the edge of the group. It is hard to believe that Stone Age artists, crouching in extremely awkward positions and mixing their colours by the flickering light of an animal-fat lamp, could have created these marvellous lifelike animals.

Although these paintings are many and are found in places hundreds of kilometres apart, certain similarities can be seen which link them. The sizes of the animals are not in proportion: a huge bison may stand next to a tiny horse. Often animals are drawn one on top of another so hiding the details of those underneath. There are no borders to the pictures but the natural curves and hollows of the rock are often used very cleverly to enhance the images painted. The animals may be painted in any orientation: upside down, sideways or the right way up. Lines, dots and geometric shapes often appear with the animals: the artists frequently placed their fingers in the paint and then made patterns of dots on the walls with their finger tips. As well as paintings, engravings are found in many of the caves.

Less well known than the cave paintings are the many small objects – decorated pebbles and pieces of carved bone or antler – that the people of the Ice Age may perhaps have carried around with them as 'lucky charms'. This piece of carved bone shows a bison licking its flank. Many of these objects were collected at the beginning of the century, when archaeologists were not always careful to record the details of their finds. As a result we do not know where many of them came from.

Some of these are exquisitely beautiful and very detailed, but like the paintings they are often engraved one on top of another so that the resulting jumble of lines makes it very difficult to see exactly what each figure was meant to represent.

Decorated bones, antlers and pebbles were also an important part of Ice Age art and these were probably carried around by the people, perhaps as 'lucky charms'. Some are little stylized female figurines. Unfortunately many of these portable objects were discovered at the beginning of the century and there is now no record of where they came from.

Mutilated hands

Hand outlines in red and black are common in many of the caves. They must have been painted by pressing a hand against the wall and then somehow spraying paint around it. This was probably done either by blowing a mouthful of paint through pursed lips, or by blowing paint down a hollow grass stalk. In one cave called Gargas, in the French Pyrenees, the walls are covered by hundreds of these hand prints, but an astonishing number show one or more of the fingers lost. In over half of them, all the fingers were lost. How these mutilations occurred we do not know, but it may have been due to some disease or perhaps frostbite in the extreme cold of the European Ice Age.

The superstitious artists

The most common animal depicted in the caves is the horse, followed by the bison and the ox. These three animals make up 60% of all the animal images. Deer, mammoth, ibex, reindeer, antelope, wild goat, wild boar, rhino, lion, hyaena, fox and wolf are occasionally found but are much less common, while birds and fish are very rare. Strangely enough, the bones found in caves where people lived tell us that reindeer and ibexes were very important food items to these artists. So why did they paint them so rarely?

Even more surprising is the scarcity of human images. The few that are found are only very sketchy outlines. If animals could be drawn in such detail then why not humans? Presumably there was some

Part of the cave wall at Gargas where the earliest artists left 'stencilled' handprints, many of which have stumps for all or some of the fingers. Experiments have shown that such prints cannot be faked by folding the fingers under the hand, so the fingers must have been missing, perhaps lost as a result of frostbite.

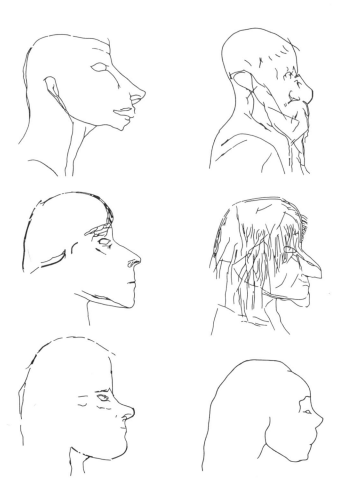

knows why the people of La Marche should have made these portraits of each other, but it is fortunate that they did, for they tell us a great deal which we would not otherwise know.

Sorcerers

In a few of the caves, a human head is drawn on an animal body. One of the most impressive of these is known as 'The Sorcerer' and is in the same cave system as the clay bison although it has to be reached by a separate entrance. 'The Sorcerer' has a deer's antlers and ears, a horse's body and tail, but human eyes, beard, legs and arms. It has been carved on a rather inaccessible part of the cave 4 metres (13 feet) above the floor. Beneath 'The Sorcerer' are hundreds of engraved animals but only 'The Sorcerer' is outlined in black paint.

It seems likely that cave art was associated with some sort of ritual. It is found in inaccessible places in the depths of caves, there are no detailed human figures, and many of the animals depicted were not normally hunted. On the other hand, animals like ibex and reindeer, that were important as food, were not often painted. All these things suggest that cave art had some sort of mystical significance.

The strange figure of the 'sorcerer' found engraved on a wall in the same cave system as the clay bison (p. 63). Several other engravings or paintings of 'sorcerers' with animal and human characteristics have been found.

A few of the engraved heads that have been found at La Marche. The portraits show that these very early people cared about their appearance, plaiting their hair or sometimes winding it up into a bun. They also wore hats, headbands and jewelry – a far cry from the conventional idea of dishevelled, brutish 'cave-men'.

sort of superstition prohibiting the depiction of human beings.

One extraordinary exception to this is the cave of La Marche in the French Pyrenees. Here 1,500 limestone blocks have been uncovered, all engraved with dozens of human faces and figures, intertwined with a mass of scratches and lines. While these faces look something like caricatures with exaggerated features, they do give us some idea of what the people looked like. A few have a muzzle-like jaw while several have upturned snub noses. Unexpectedly, more of the heads have short hair than long, and several have 'pudding-basin' hair styles with a fringe. Fine plaiting appears on some and even what looks like a bun. There are ten beards and a few moustaches. One headband shows up clearly and there are several hats, belts and bracelets. No one

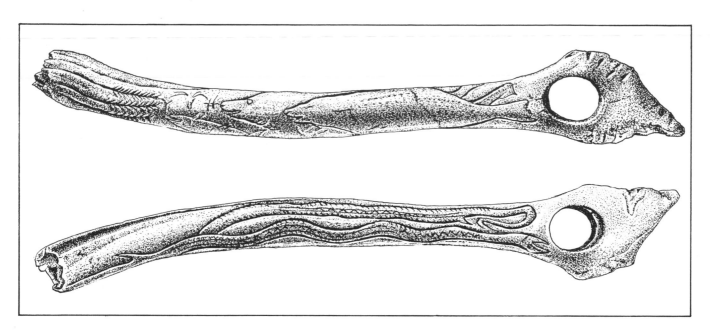

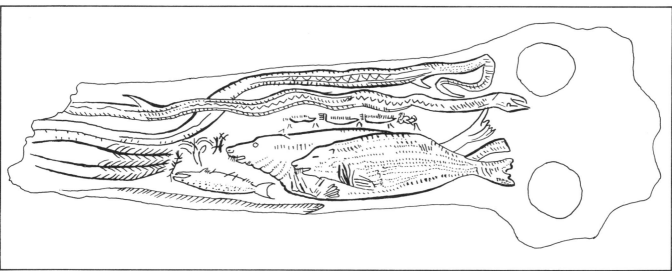

Recording the seasons

Modern hunting tribes name the months of the year
according to natural events such as the calving of
reindeer, the rutting of moose and the migration of
birds. Some of the portable objects show events
typical of certain seasons which may mean that early
man had a similar 'calendar'. A small bone knife that
has clearly never been used to cut anything has
engravings on the blade which could represent
spring and autumn. On one side is a doe, wavy lines
indicating water, three flowers in spring bloom and
an ibex head with one horn crossed out. On the other
side is the head of a bison bull bellowing in the
autumn rut, some leafless branches, some nuts and a
dying flower. An even more vivid spring scene is
engraved around the curved section of a reindeer
antler found at Montgaudier in France. A male and
female seal swim next to a salmon with a hook on its
lower jaw, typical of male salmon when they swim
upstream to mate. Two snakes lie alongside each
other, while stems with leaves and a tiny flower add
more detail to this delicately carved spring scene.

Europe in the Ice Age

To begin to understand European cave art we need
to know what Europe was like at the time. Ice fields

and glaciers covered Scandinavia and most of Britain, while south of these was treeless tundra and steppe, where reindeer, mammoths, woolly rhinoceroses, musk oxen and horses were plentiful. In southern France, the climate was less severe, and in the low-lying hills and valleys, ibexes, chamois, wild boars, deer and the gigantic Irish elks roamed. Lions, leopards, wolves and foxes preyed on all these herbivores, while salmon, pike, trout and eels were plentiful in the rivers.

In spite of the enormous number of animals, the human population was sparse, probably only a few tens of thousands. These people led a wandering life, moving from place to place in search of food. They followed the migrating herds of reindeer or bison for hundreds of kilometres, collecting nuts, berries and small animals wherever they could. Their lives were probably governed by the movements of the reindeer. Herds of reindeer spend a large part of the year on the move. Each spring a herd gathers together to make the journey to its summer feeding grounds, and in the autumn they congregate again to travel to their winter feeding grounds. We can assume that the reindeer of the Ice Age followed a similar pattern. To be sure of keeping a regular supply of meat, the people had to follow them, returning year after year to the same camp-sites along the route.

The artists of Africa

Prehistoric art is only found where there were suitable rock surfaces to be painted, and where conditions since then have preserved the paintings. In Europe, the deep caves have preserved many cave paintings undamaged. Although cave art of this time is also known from Africa, it is less well preserved.

In the 1950s my parents spent several years recording the art of rock shelters in central Tanzania. In this area there are many large rock faces which presented ideal surfaces for painting. But unfortunately they are exposed to the sun, wind and rain, and much of the art is now very faded. These paintings were originally considered to be fairly recent,

At about the same time that the artists of Lascaux and Altamira were at work, others were painting on rock shelters in the warmer climate of Africa. These people did not have the same reluctance to portray human beings and their paintings tell us a lot about Stone Age life. Here we see a lion and various other animals, including giraffe, eland and kudu. In the midst of these animals, a group of people appear to be taking part in a dance or some kind of ceremony.

and related to those of the !Kung San found in southern Africa, but comparison of the styles shows this cannot be so. And in an excavation at one of the sites, shaped artist's colouring materials were found 7.5 metres (25 feet) below the surface, in a layer that was dated at 35,000 years. This shows that artists were at work in Africa at approximately the same time as in Europe.

My parents spent long hours recording these paintings in Tanzania. They would erect some sort of scaffolding and then trace the paintings onto cellophane stuck onto the rock surface using coloured pens. Then they would copy the tracings onto art paper and carefully match the colours against the originals. Finally they would make a scaled down plan of the paintings on graph paper. In the eighty-eight sites they recorded they were able to recognize a number of very distinct styles superimposed on earlier styles.

Several of the Tanzanian paintings show daily scenes: a group of women bathing in a river, a stick dance and an elephant in a trap. The animals are clearly recognizable with eland, gazelle, giraffe, rhino and elephant being the most commonly drawn. Humans are drawn but they are always stylized in contrast to the lifelike animals. They are also drawn in two different ways – either with a solid football-shaped head or with an elaborate head-dress. The former may be women and the latter men, or they may be different styles associated with different periods of time. As with the European cave art the beauty, simplicity and life in these paintings is quite unique.

The artists disappear

A problem with cave art is that it is not easy to date. Rarely is a painting associated with an excavation. It is only by matching styles of paintings with engraved bones and stones or characteristic colouring material from dated levels, that the age can be estimated. But we do know that cave art in Europe suddenly vanished about 10,000 years ago as the climate began to warm at the end of the Ice Age. Its disappearance seems to be associated with an important change in the way of life of the people. After this time, we begin to get evidence that instead of wandering from place to place finding food by hunting and gathering, people in different parts of the world were gradually beginning to settle down and become farmers. They were learning to grow plants and domesticate animals, and for the first time they lived in one place for several generations.

Chapter Ten

The hunter settles down

The beginnings of pastoralism

How did the change to a settled way of life come about? It is generally agreed that this occurred quite quickly about 10,000 years ago with the development of crop farming. Pastoralism, the herding of animals, appears to have developed more gradually and could have its roots as far back as 30,000 years ago. The evidence for this is rather interesting and we will take a closer look at it.

In 1910, a French prehistorian discovered some front teeth of a horse which were worn down in an unusual way. He recognized that they could have been worn away as a result of 'crib-biting', a behaviour occasionally displayed by tethered horses. These horses arch their necks, press their teeth into a hard surface such as a post or stable door and breath in deeply. Most vets think they do it out of boredom, but it can make them seriously ill. Apart from this, crib-biting wears the front teeth into a chisel shape.

This carved horse-head was found in a French cave known as St Michel d'Arudy in 1893. It seems to show a bridle made of rope, but most prehistorians dismissed these marks as insignificant decoration until 1966, when another horse-head, with a bridle unmistakably marked, was found at La Marche.

The amazing thing about the worn-down, fossilized horse teeth found in France was that they were 30,000 years old. Naturally no one believed that horses were tethered such a long time ago as this, and the idea was soon forgotten, but now people are beginning to take it seriously.

On many engravings of horse heads found in Ice Age sites, the prehistoric artist has drawn lines around the muzzle which look exactly like bridles. In the past, these lines were dismissed as muscle markings or insignificant decorations. But in 1966, a horse's head was found at a site in France called La Marche which was about 15,000 years old. This engraving had the unmistakable outline of a halter made of twisted rope carved over the animal's head. With this new evidence, people are beginning to look again at some of the other engravings: they now think that these too may show bridles.

Another clue which suggests that people had some control over horses is the presence of numerous carefully carved batons in a number of sites. These are usually curved, and are shaped in the form of a T or Y. They have one or two holes carved in one end and these holes show signs of wear by a soft material such as leather. Many ideas have been suggested for the purpose of these batons: one is that they were used as the solid cheek pieces of a horse's harness.

Controlling animal herds

Apart from the tethering of horses, it also seems that, after 30,000 years ago, there was controlled hunting of large herds of animals. At many sites the bones of one type of animal are far more numerous than any

In the north of Norway, Lapps still follow the reindeer herds, controlling their movements by a variety of ingenious methods. Here a tethered reindeer is led across a stream by boat, causing the rest of the herd to follow. Recent evidence suggests that our early ancestors may have controlled reindeer herds in a similar way.

other bones. Some sites in the French Pyrenees are full of reindeer bones, while others have almost nothing but ibex. Gazelles abound in early Israeli sites and at the foot of a cliff at Solutré in France thousands of horses were found. Maybe the people who killed these animals used some of the same hunting tricks that Laplanders use today. Lapp hunters have found ways of controlling the reindeer herds rather than having to follow them everywhere they go. One of the things they do is to drive the reindeer into a valley and then camp at the entrance so that the animals are effectively trapped. Some of the caves inhabited by Ice Age hunters overlook the narrow entrances of valleys and may have served just this purpose.

The Laplanders also have another trick. They catch a few reindeer, put them into bridles, and tie them up. The rest of the herd will not desert the tethered animals and are, again, effectively kept in one place. Maybe the curiously shaped batons already described were also used to tether reindeer. And perhaps the thousands of horses at Solutré were driven against the cliff and so trapped. All these clues do suggest that the people had a certain amount of control of the animals and may have been herding them at least for some of the time.

So it may be that, for several thousand years, Ice Age people had some control over herds of wild horses, reindeer and ibexes instead of just hunting them at random. But what about agriculture? How did the wandering hunter-gatherers learn to plant crops and gather and store their harvests?

Climate may be the clue

As the last Ice Age drew to a close, the weather warmed up and the glaciers began to melt. The sea level rose by 130 metres (430 feet) and flooded much of the land. One-twentieth of the land surface of the world disappeared under the sea. The North Sea and the English Channel were formed and the map of Europe began to look much as it does today.

As acres of pasture disappeared under the sea, the reindeer began to return once more to their northern homelands. Meanwhile the warm springs and summers began to turn the remaining plains into woods and meadows. Larch and birch trees began to grow, then, later, ash and oak trees. Short, coarse grass gave way to bushes and flowers, and between the patches of woodland, tall, waving grasses began to appear. With the woodland and meadows came new sorts of animals: asses, oxen and deer now grazed where once great herds of reindeer had gathered.

Winter camp at Duruthy

One site in France called Duruthy tells us a little about the way of life of the people at the time of this change in climate. Here, 9,500 years ago, between September and February each year, people gathered in a sort of village. In the autumn they lived on salmon which they speared with bone harpoons, and in the winter reindeer formed their staple diet. These people were very skilled craftsmen and they left behind some 10,000 beautifully worked flint tools. Some of these were very tiny bladelets which probably formed part of a sickle. They have glue adhering to the blunt edge and a polish on the sharp edge which is characteristic of tools used to cut grasses. A row of these tiny blades were probably stuck into a wooden or bone handle to make a sickle. There are also stones found at Duruthy which look as if they were used to grind seeds into flour. These people probably harvested wild grasses and made them into some sort of bread or porridge to supplement their winter diet of reindeer meat. In the next section we will see how a way of life such as this may have developed into a settled, agricultural existence.

The beginnings of agriculture

Agriculture seems to have developed independently in several major centres in the world. There is the area called the Fertile Crescent which lies to the east of the Mediterranean Sea, where 10,000 years ago the change in climate led to the spread of wild cereals. Here the staple diet was wheat and barley. In northeast China the staple diet was millet approximately 7,000 years ago, but later rice and soya beans were also domesticated. In the New World, agriculture began over 6,000 years ago with the growing of maize in Mexico. These early maize farmers also grew squash (marrow-like vegetables) and beans. Further south in the Andes Mountains, the potato was brought under cultivation. The evidence for Africa is incomplete, but we know that sorghum, yams, peanuts and several different types of millet were domesticated there. While different foods formed the staple in each major centre, the original change to a settled life seems to have come initially through the harvesting and storing of wild crops and planting followed from this.

In the Fertile Crescent we are fairly certain that the first step towards agriculture was a settled way of life where people harvested the plentiful wild grasses. One of the earliest sites we know of, where people were harvesting wild cereals, is Abu Hureya in Syria. Here, between 11,500 and 10,000 years ago, people gathered a wild wheat, called einkorn, wild barley and rye. The tools needed to utilize grass seeds – sickles and grinding stones – have been found in this ancient village. The village litter shows that the inhabitants were also hunting rabbits, gazelle, sheep, goats and wild asses, catching fish and gathering shellfish, wild lentils, nuts and berries. But, unlike earlier hunter-gatherers, they were able to find enough food to form a permanent village settlement.

To prove that it would have been possible to live on wild cereals in the Fertile Crescent, one scientist decided to see how long it would take to harvest the einkorn which still grows wild in the area today. Using only a 9,000-year-old flint sickle, he harvested 3 kilograms (6 pounds) of grain in one hour. He calculated from this that a family, even if they worked fairly slowly, would have been able to harvest more wild wheat in three weeks than they could eat in a year.

A stone pestle-and-mortar found in Israel may have been used to grind wild cereals as long as 10,000 years ago. The flour that resulted was probably cooked into a porridge or made into unleavened bread. In the Fertile Crescent, wild cereals grew so thickly that our ancestors could collect enough food to settle in one place.

Wild wheat such as this still covers the less arid parts of the Middle East today. At first our ancestors simply reaped the wild wheat and continued to hunt animals and gather other plant foods. Within a few thousand years, however, they began to sow their own cereals and thus true farming began.

The wheat changes

In many villages in the Middle East, the change from gathering wild wheat to cultivating wheat seems to have happened about 10,000 years ago. We can tell when wild wheat began to be planted because the wheat itself changed. When wild wheat is ripe, the seeds fall from the stem onto the ground, but there are a few mutants (see p. 8) in wild wheat where the seeds remain firmly attached to the stem. As the people harvested wild wheat, they would have tended to collect more of the seeds which were firmly attached than the loose ones. Because these characteristics are passed on in the genes (see p. 7) once they started planting their own seed, they would grow far more mutant plants with firmly attached seeds than plants with loose seeds. In this way the wheat began to change, so that now, domesticated wheat differs from wild wheat in having the ripe seeds firmly attached to the stem in *all* plants.

10,000 years ago in the Fertile Crescent, wild wheat grew thickly on the plains and hillsides. With this abundant source of food, people were able to give up their nomadic existence and settle permanently in one place. If we could go back in time, this is the scene we might see as all the members of a village helped to bring in the rich harvest of grain.

Salinas de Chao

A settled way of life first developed in the Fertile Crescent because natural food resources were plentiful, and a similar chain of events happened on the coastal plain of Peru. Here, 4,000 years ago, there was a large community, possibly as many as 2,000 people, at Salinas de Chao. The site was then on the coast but is now 3 kilometres (2 miles) inland because the land has risen. In the sand dunes at Salinas de Chao are enormous numbers of anchovy bones, the bones of deepwater fish, and the remains of shellfish. It is clear that these people obtained their food from the sea. They also grew bottle gourds and cotton which provided floats and mesh for their nets. They presumably ate the contents of the gourds, and the squash, which they also grew. Dozens of similar settled communities developed along the Peruvian coast showing that with a rich food resource, large settled communities could thrive without agriculture. The people of Salinas de Chao lived like this for hundreds of years, but eventually they moved inland, abandoned their fishing, and became full-time farmers.

Not everyone settled down

Although, 10,000 years ago, groups of people settled down in villages and towns and many of our ancestors started to become farmers, others did not. Many of the American Indians, until very recently, still lived by hunting the huge herds of bison that roamed the country. Some Eskimos in the cold north still hunt seals, bears and fish, although most have given up this way of life. In Australia, the aborigines lived by hunting kangaroos and bandicoots and used to fish the lakes for golden perch and freshwater cod, while in southern Africa some of the !Kung San continue to practise a hunting-and-gathering way of life. Many nomadic tribes such as the Maasai and the Turkana people in East Africa live by herding cattle, goats or camels, and until very recently seldom practised any form of agriculture. This is now all changing, but only in the past few years.

These Txicao Indians from South America are some of the few remaining hunter-gatherers in the world. They sleep in hammocks and have few other possessions. Only when human beings settled in one place and began to collect material goods did serious, organized aggression begin.

The seeds of aggression

So it was only in certain parts of the world that agriculture thrived, and in these places towns and cities grew and a fundamental change in social values and behaviour took place. Hunter-gatherers are very generous people. Their possessions are few and they share everything they have, knowing that it can be readily replaced. But when people settle down it is different. Their possessions multiply; they need axes and saws to cut down trees for building, ploughs to break the ground, hoes to weed, sickles to harvest, baskets to carry the crop and barns to store it in. All these things are essential to grow even the simplest crops. Moreover, the food grown each year has to last until the following year so it has to be stored safely. The land, the possessions and the stored food are all essential for the livelihood of agricultural people and they are protected and defended against any unwelcome intruder. I believe that this is how the first seeds of aggression were sown.

The population explosion

Aggression among modern populations is increasing and every day we hear of violent incidents. One reason for this is our rapidly expanding population which results in serious overcrowding. Normally the number of individuals in an animal population is controlled by natural checks such as the amount of food available, diseases, parasites and predators. If these natural checks are removed the animal population will increase at an accelerating pace and we humans are no exception to this rule.

Ten thousand years ago there were probably about ten million people in the world, all living by hunting-and-gathering. With the development of agriculture more food became available and the number of people began to rise. By 2,000 years ago it is estimated that the world population had increased to 300 million. This increase continued and has been further accelerated by the development of modern medicine which enables us to cure many diseases. There are now 4,000 million people in the world and it is thought that by the year 2000 this number will be 6,000 million.

The arms boom

Today the world is divided by two principle opposing philosophies. One of these, the capitalist philosophy, is based on private enterprise, where individuals are free to create their own wealth from capital and where they own as much property and have as many possessions as they can afford. The other is the socialist philosophy, where the community as a whole benefits from any wealth created. Each individual works for the community and every individual in the community benefits. The state provides for each person's wants: free medical care, free education and security in old age. Most countries in the world have systems of government that are based on one or other of these philosophies but with many variations.

The differences between these two systems of government are so fundamental that suspicion, distrust and tension have developed between the world's largest and most powerful nations. And because the rest of the world is encouraged to follow one or other, these tensions have spread throughout the world. The result is a frightening increase in the number and destructive power of modern weapons. Modern nuclear arsenals have a total explosive power of one million Hiroshima bombs. The United States of America and Russia have a total of 16,000 nuclear warheads between them, enough to destroy every one of the 400 major cities in the northern hemisphere *forty* times each. If the governments concerned explode only a fraction of all this, the earth would be devastated and all forms of life extinguished forever.

A variety of cultures

As well as these ideological differences, the modern world is divided by the many different cultural traditions of its people. Yet none of these differences should divide us, since all these things are learned, not inherited. When we are born we do not know or believe anything. We have a very long childhood, during which time we learn to live in the society into which we were born. We learn the rules, traditions and beliefs. The way we behave in adult life depends very much on what we have learned during this time. If we are born into a Muslim community, we will learn Muslim traditions and beliefs, while if we are born into a Catholic community we will learn to be Catholics. If we grow up in Russia we will believe that communism is best, but if we grow up in America we will believe that capitalism is best. There are so many traditions and beliefs, who can say that one is right and better than another? What is important is to realize that through communication, be it books, radio, television or travel, we can all learn to understand and respect one another.

The books we read and the films we watch should promote this sort of understanding. Yet many of the programmes shown on television and the stories told in novels are predominantly about violence. So many films are about wars and murders that we may see literally hundreds of people killed on the television screen every week. All this must surely encourage us to be aggressive. It would be much better if there were more non-violent films that showed us the variety and richness of our world and its people. It is only by understanding other people's traditions and customs that future generations can hope to live together peacefully.

Learning from each other

We can all benefit from a knowledge and understanding of other people's ways of life. For example, technological development has taken place at different rates in different parts of the world, and those in the less developed countries can learn from the experience of those in the more advanced countries. The rapid development of technology has brought many benefits, but it has also brought problems. The price for an easier life has been pollution and the destruction of the environment. Developed nations have lost most of their wild animals and many of their plants, because the natural habitat has had to make way for technological development. A manmade, concrete world, without any wild animals or natural places, should not be all we leave for future generations. Development must be planned to avoid unnecessary destruction and waste.

Those in the more technological societies may also have something to learn from those in less industrialized societies. In the rushed and competitive life of modern cities, people often have no time for their less fortunate friends and relatives. When parents become old and unable to look after themselves, their children put them in a home to be looked after by strangers rather than by those they love. When a friend is ill, people have no time to help out. A look at the more relaxed rural communities around the world, where family ties and friendships remain strong and meaningful, is a reminder of what the busy, modern city-dweller has lost. A world without love and compassion is not one we should encourage.

Rich man, poor man

I have talked about the variety in traditions and cultures of human societies, and how these add to the richness of the world. But there is one fundamental factor which *does* divide the world and which requires all our efforts and understanding to resolve. This is the difference between the rich and the poor nations.

Aggression is something we are taught, not an indelible part of human nature. In the early 1970s a tribe known as the Tasaday were discovered living in caves in a remote and mountainous region of the Philippines. They never fought among themselves and did not kill for food since they thought of the animals of the forest as their friends. The Tasaday are a living demonstration of our basic nature, for we are fundamentally sociable and co-operative creatures – this is how we have survived up to now and it is the key to our future. The modern trend towards violence, in films, on television and in books, is a harmful one for it encourages us to be aggressive.

For those of us who live in warm, dry houses with running water, electricity and a plentiful supply of food it is hard to imagine living without these things. But only one-quarter of the world's population has these advantages. These rich people in the developed nations consume four-fifths of the world's food, fuel and other resources. Three-quarters of the world's population are found in the developing countries where they live a precarious existence on the remaining one-fifth of the world's resources.

Imagine having to collect your water from a river or water hole and carry it several miles to your home. Imagine not having gas or electricity to light your home or cook your food. Imagine depending for food largely on the crops that you grow, and the cattle, sheep and goats that you herd. Imagine how it must feel to know that your source of food is never guaranteed. It can vanish with drought, floods, or other natural disasters, and then you and your family starve.

One consequence of such an uncertain lifestyle is that people try to create more security by having a large family. Children can help to herd the cattle, collect the water, and harvest the grain. They will also take care of their parents in old age. Some may even find factory jobs and support the rest of the family in times of hardship. Of course, a lot of food is needed to feed all these children but people living in such poor conditions still tend to have large families to ensure that someone will take care of them when they get old. As a result, population growth is greatest in the least developed parts of the world. Modern medicine now ensures that about half of the children born will grow up – considerably more than in the past. But the lack of food means that they are often undernourished. It is a vicious circle which can only be broken by raising the living standards of these people, so that life holds some real security, other than that provided by the family.

The right sort of aid

The developed nations of the world try to help the less developed nations by giving them aid. But all too often most of this 'aid' is in the form of guns, tanks and fighter jets. In many other cases foreign assistance is provided in the form of loans to develop an industry. Usually this is an industry from which the donor country will benefit. Thus schemes are introduced to mine rare minerals, or to grow cash crops such as coffee, pineapples or cut-flowers. These products are then exported to the developed world at very low prices.

What is most needed is massive financial assistance in the form of grants for agricultural development. This would enable the less privileged three-quarters of the world's population to raise their standard of living, and so halt the continuing growth of the world population.

The world's resources are probably insufficient to support even the present population, if everyone practised the lavish lifestyle of the wealthier nations. By the year 2000 there will be six billion people alive, and the world's resources could certainly not support such a lifestyle for all of them. However, if the present unfair situation continues, the inevitable result will be global conflicts, because the majority of the world's people will demand their share of the world's wealth.

The future

The future of the human race may look bleak with the threat of nuclear war, increasing racial violence, rising population numbers, mass starvation and the rapid destruction of the environment. Yet we are the most intelligent species alive today, and I am sure that with greater understanding and co-operation, and with a willingness to share resources, we can make the world a better place for future generations everywhere. But we must work together. It is no longer just our house, our city, our land, or even our country that we have to defend. It is our world.

We can now send people, instruments, and laboratories into outer space to investigate the distant planets. From this perspective we can see the world as a whole – a relatively small planet with limited resources and a natural balance which is easily upset. The knowledge of the limitations of our world should unite us in a common goal to preserve what we possess. As we have shared our past, so shall we share our future.

Further reading

Evolution, Colin Patterson
(British Museum, Natural History, London, 1978)
A clear and simple account of modern knowledge about evolution, well illustrated with photographs and diagrams.

The Illustrated Origin of Species, Charles Darwin, Abridged and Introduced by Richard E. Leakey
(Faber and Faber, London, 1979; Hill and Wang, New York, 1979)
An abridged version of Darwin's classic with notes and an introduction to bring the text up-to-date; numerous illustrations help to explain his arguments about natural selection and 'the survival of the fittest'.

Leakey's Luck, The Life of Louis Leakey 1903–72, Sonia Cole
(Collins, London, 1975)
A good biography of Louis, which also explains the significance of the discoveries he and Mary Leakey made.

Olduvai Gorge: My Search for Early Man, Mary D. Leakey
(Collins, London, 1979)
A fascinating account of almost fifty years' work at the world's richest prehistoric site.

The Evolution of Early Man, Bernard Wood
(Peter Lowe, London, 1978)
A good account of human evolution, well illustrated with many helpful diagrams.

Secrets of the Ice Age, Evan Haddingham
(Heinemann, London, 1980)
A detailed look at the mysterious people of the Ice Age, who created the magnificent paintings at Lascaux and may have begun to tame animals such as the horse and the reindeer.

Farming in Prehistory: from Hunter-Gatherer to Food Producer, Barbara Bender
(J. Baker, London, 1975)
This book describes how our ancestors became farmers, one of the most significant steps in the history of mankind.

How the Other Half Dies: The Real Reasons for World Hunger, Susan George
(Penguin, London, 1977; Allenheld, Osmun & Co., New York, 1977)
A good analysis of the true causes of poverty and malnutrition in the Third World.

Glossary

adapted Fitted to a particular environment as a result of the process of natural selection (*qv*).

amphibians A group of animals that includes the frogs, toads, newts and salamanders.

anthropology The study of the human species; palaeoanthropology includes the study of extinct hominids.

apes A group of animals that includes the gorilla, chimpanzee, orang-utan, gibbon and siamang. The first three are often called the 'great apes'.

archaeology The study of prehistoric remains.

australopithecines A group of early hominids that are so different from human beings that they are placed in a different genus. *See also*: gracile australopithecines, robust australopithecines.

Australopithecus The genus (*qv*) to which all australopithecines belong.

Australopithecus afarensis The name given to a group of hominids over three million years old, found at Hadar in Ethiopia and at Laetoli in Tanzania. Not everyone agrees that these all belong to the same species.

Australopithecus africanus The scientific name for gracile australopithecines (*qv*).

Australopithecus boisei The scientific name for the robust australopithecines (*qv*) found in East Africa.

Australopithecus robustus The scientific name for the robust australopithecines (*qv*) found in South Africa.

bipedal Walking on two legs as the usual means of locomotion.

brow-ridge A ridge of bone that juts out above the eye.

carnivore A meat-eating animal.

Cro-Magnon Man A name often used for prehistoric finds that belong to the species *Homo sapiens sapiens*.

dryopithecines An extinct group of apes; there were many different species of dryopithecines and they varied a great deal in size.

evolution The process by which successive generations of animals and plants gradually change, over long periods of time.

flint A hard, glassy, sedimentary rock (*qv*) that is especially useful for making stone tools. It is found as nodules that are white on the outside and dark grey inside.

fossil Any remains or signs of living things preserved in the earth. The term fossil includes such things as insect remains, footprints and leaf impressions, but is most often used for bones that have been preserved by a chemical process in the soil. This process, known as fossilization, literally turns them into rock, replacing their natural substance with minerals, but preserving their exact shape and even their texture.

gene A unit of heredity; a single 'instruction' among the set of genetic instructions that parents pass on to their offspring.

genus A group of species that are closely related to each other. The first part of a scientific name (*eg Homo, Australopithecus*) refers to the genus, while the second part describes the species.

geology The study of the rocks of the earth and the processes by which they have been formed.

gracile australopithecines Small hominids of slight build who lived in Africa about two million years ago. They had fairly small brains and probably did not make tools.

herbivores Animals that eat only plants.

hominid Creatures that were more human-like than ape-like. This term includes humans themselves, all other species of *Homo*, and all species of *Australopithecus*.

Homo The genus (*qv*) to which humans and the immediate ancestors of humans belong.

Homo erectus A hominid that lived from about one-and-a-half million years ago until 300,000 years ago. Although physically fairly similar to modern humans, the brain of this hominid was smaller than ours and its face was different, having very heavy brow-ridges.

Homo habilis A hominid that lived about two million years ago, at the same time as the australopithecines (*qv*). This hominid had a larger brain than the australopithecines (although smaller than the brain of its successor *Homo erectus*) and made stone tools.

Homo sapiens Biologically modern man. The species includes two subspecies: *Homo sapiens neanderthalensis* Neandertal Man, and *Homo sapiens sapiens* fully modern man. Only *Homo sapiens sapiens* is alive today.

hunter-gatherers People that live by hunting wild animals and gathering edible wild plants.

Ice Ages Periods when the earth was very much colder than it is today and glaciers covered much of northern Eurasia and North America. There have been seven such periods in the last two million years. The last Ice Age began about 70,000 years ago and had ended by about 10,000 years ago.

limestone A white sedimentary rock (*qv*) that is slightly soluble in rainwater, and thus tends to dissolve to form underground caves.

mammals Warm-blooded animals that generally have fur covering their bodies (exceptions include whales, seals, pigs, rhinoceroses and elephants), give birth to live young (exceptions are spiny anteaters and the duck-billed platypus), and suckle their young with milk.

mutant An animal or plant that carries a mutation (*qv*).

mutation A change in a gene (*qv*) that results in a new characteristic (*ie* a characteristic that had not been seen in the parents or any earlier generations) appearing in the offspring.

natural selection The process which Charles Darwin proposed to account for evolution (*qv*). It depends on the fact that some animals or plants do better in life than others, so passing on more of their genes (*qv*) to the next generation.

Neandertal Man A stockily built type of *Homo sapiens* (*qv*) that lived in Europe and parts of Asia between about 100,000 years ago and 30,000 years ago. This partly coincided with the last Ice Age, and Neandertal Man may have adapted to severe cold weather.

palaeoanthropology *See:* anthropology.

palaeontology The study of the fossils of extinct animals and plants.

pastoralism The keeping of herds of domesticated animals.

pollen A very light, powdery substance produced by plants for the purpose of cross-fertilization.

prehistory The period of human existence before anyone began to record events, *ie* before history.

primates A group of mammals that includes lemurs, lorises, bushbabies, monkeys, apes and hominids (*qv*).

quartz A hard, glass-like mineral.

Ramapithecus An ape-like creature that lived from about fourteen million years ago until at least eight million years ago, possibly longer. It may have been the ancestor of the hominids.

ramapithecines A group of ape-like animals that lived in open woodland in Europe, Asia and Africa over eight million years ago. They varied greatly in size. Some may have been ancestral to the apes and some ancestral to the hominids.

reptiles A group of animals that includes the snakes, lizards, turtles, tortoises and crocodiles.

robust australopithecines Heavily built but small-brained hominids that lived in Africa about two million years ago. They probably did not make tools. The male was larger than the female and had exceptionally large teeth and jaws.

savanna Open grassland with scattered trees and bushes. Savanna is the typical vegetation of East Africa.

sedimentary rock Rock that has been formed through the build-up of sediments, usually where lakes or rivers deposit gravel, sand or mud.

selection *See:* natural selection.

species A group of animals that can all interbreed one with another to produce fertile offspring. Because they can freely interbreed they usually all look very similar.

stereoscopic vision Vision that allows depth and distance to be estimated.

tool-kit The full range of tools typical of a particular period in time or a particular hominid.

tundra The vegetation of sub-arctic regions where, owing to the cold, only mosses, lichens and grasses will grow.

Illustration acknowledgments

6 Anthony Maynard
8 (left) Richard Wrangham/Anthrophoto
8 (right) The Times/Camera Press
9 Ron Bowen
10 Ron Bowen
11 Irven DeVore/Anthrophoto
12 Michael Woods
13 Granville Davies
14 Eugene Fleury
16 Nicholas Hall
17 (bottom) Dr Patrick Echlin/Science Photo Library
20 Ron Bowen
21 Ron Bowen
22 Eugene Fleury
23 Stewart Halperin/Tom Stack
24 Bob Campbell
25 The Cleveland Museum of Natural History
26 Ron Bowen
27 Ron Bowen
29 Ron Bowen
32 Ron Bowen
38–9 Ron Bowen
41 Washburn/Anthrophoto
47 Eugene Fleury
48 British Museum (Natural History)
50 Marion Appelton
51 Ron Bowen
52 (top) Von Puttkamer/Alan Hutchinson
52 (bottom) Napoleon Chagnon/Anthrophoto
55 The Illustrated London News
56 (top) Joyce Tuhill
56 (bottom) Nicholas Hall. Adapted from *Ice-Age Hunters of the Ukraine,*
    Richard G. Klein. Copyright © 1974 by Scientific American Inc. All rights reserved.
58–9 Ron Bowen
60 Eugene Fleury
61 Nicholas DeVore/Bruce Coleman Ltd.
63 (top) Begouën Collection, photo: Jean Vertut
63 (bottom) Jean Vertut
65 Jean Vertut
66 (top) Nicholas Hall, after Professor Léon Pales, courtesy Editions Ophrys.
66 (bottom) Martin Bronkhorst
67 Joyce Tuhill, after Alexander Marshack
70 Musée des Antiquités Nationales, Paris
71 Brian and Cherry Alexander
74–5 Ron Bowen
76 Alan Hutchinson
79 J. Nance/John Hillelson Agency

The photographs on the following pages were taken by Pete Kain (© Richard Leakey):
17 (top), 18 (top and bottom), 19, 21, 22, 27, 28, 29, 30, 31, 33, 34, 35, 37,
40 (top and bottom), 42, 43 (left and right), 44, 45, 46, 49 (top, centre
and bottom), 53, 54, 64, 68, 73 (top and bottom).

Index

Numbers in *italic* refer to illustrations